*ten*minute
pilates

Joyce Gavin & Walter McKone

**BARNES
& NOBLE**

NEW YORK

This edition published
by Barnes & Noble Publishing, Inc.,
by arrangement with Parragon Publishing.

2004 Barnes & Noble Books

M 10 9 8 7 6 5 4 3 2

ISBN: 0-7607-5026-2

Copyright © 2004 by Parragon Books Ltd

Printed and bound in Indonesia
Produced by the Bridgewater Book Company Ltd.

Contents

Introduction

The Pilates approach offers you a gentle but powerful pathway to achieving your natural potential for health, strength, flexibility, and stamina. Developed in the early 20th century, this unique and increasingly popular form of exercise can help you to develop supple movements and strength as well as improve your posture and general well-being.

Whether practiced intensely over an hour or in more manageable ten-minute sessions, the Pilates approach combines working on the body's muscle groups with maintaining smooth, flowing movements, a strong, centered posture, breath control, and clear mental focus.

The system was developed by Joseph H. Pilates. Pilates had been a sickly child but had used physical exercise to improve his health and physique. A German by birth, he moved to England in 1912, where he became a boxer. However, when World War I broke out, being an immigrant he found himself interned on the Isle of Wight. Pilates passed his time by teaching other internees how to promote their physical fitness. He soon developed his first piece of exercise equipment, the so-called "Universal Reformer," made from the springs of a hospital bed and used to help patients work out as they lay in bed. Pilates found that spinal-injury patients recovered more quickly when they used his equipment and this stimulated his lifelong interest in remedial exercise.

The Pilates exercises taught in this book may differ from those created by Joseph Pilates, but they still adhere to the basic principles of focusing the mind and relaxing and stabilizing the body while you exercise.

Mind and body

After the war, Pilates moved to the United States and opened a fitness center in New York. His classes became particularly popular with dancers, who identified with his emphasis on flowing movement and mental focus. Pilates continued to develop his system throughout his lifetime, studying different sports as well as yoga and the animal world to increase his instinctive understanding of the body. In addition, he adapted his exercises to the needs of individual students. Since his death, his students have developed the practice further and there is no one set way of teaching Pilates. However, an intentional mind–body interaction is one of the basic keys to the Pilates approach, wherever and however it is taught.

Pilates movement

Practicing Pilates regularly for just ten minutes at a time will help you to develop core stability and strength. This increases your movement control and helps you to retain a relaxed but strong posture.

neck and shoulders free from tension

back straight but relaxed

strong abdomen

centered pelvis

weight centered on the feet to provide a solid foundation

who can use this *book?*

The Pilates approach to exercise set out in this book can be followed by almost anyone, of any age. Since the exercises are gentle, and your sessions will be short, any strain on the body is at a minimum. This reduces the risks of injury during and after exercising. Pilates movements reach deep into the body, stimulating good muscle development and a more effective circulation.

Because it encourages you to work slowly and at your own pace, almost anyone can practice Pilates. Most people begin with simple exercises and build up to more advanced techniques, depending on their fitness levels and ability. Even if you don't have ten minutes practice time to spare, you can incorporate the Pilates approach into everyday activities and other forms of exercise you already practice.

   The exercises in this book are relatively simple and are aimed at providing an introduction to Pilates for people who have reasonable health and are injury-free.

Practiced correctly and regularly, these exercises can help you to improve your physical and mental well-being in various ways. For example, if you write, use a computer, or drive for long periods, your muscles are likely to tire and, in turn, your posture will suffer. The exercises will help you to strengthen muscle and tissue tone, to give you better support and stability.

Using this book

Although this is a practical book, it is recommended that you read it through before trying the exercises. This will help you to understand the fundamental elements of Pilates and vital safety points, which will help you to do the exercises correctly.

   Perform the exercises a few at a time so that you assimilate the Pilates approach slowly and methodically. Don't try to do too many exercises at once as your focus and efficiency will be reduced if you get tired. Ten minutes in the morning and ten minutes in the evening is ideal, but this might not be possible every day. Practice two to three times a week if you can.

   This book is not intended as a substitute for taking classes with a Pilates trainer, who can help you understand the principles more fully.

You can take up Pilates at any stage of life. Keeping your mental focus will ensure you remain aware of how your body feels, which will help you to exercise safely.

what *ten-minutes pilates* can do for you

better flexibility Pilates helps you to develop flexibility, which in turn improves the range of your movements and the shock-absorbing efficiency of your body. Over time, your movement patterns will become more fluid, allowing you to move with less effort and more grace.

improved strength Your strength will increase as the stability of your muscles and joints improves and you learn how to move and use your body more effectively and efficiently.

increased muscle tone Stretching in the Pilates way enhances the tone of your muscles without promoting ungainly muscle growth. Good muscle tone provides the body with structural support at all times, even when you are at rest.

improves your circulation The coordination of slow movements and breathing improves blood circulation to particular parts of the body. Different Pilates exercises work specifically to stimulate the circulation to areas of the body that are under your control. Better circulation improves general health.

deeper, more efficient breathing One of the essential elements of Pilates is improving your breathing. Better breathing improves oxygen supply and helps to remove carbon dioxide build-up from your muscles.

greater oxygen supply to the blood As a consequence of better breathing, oxygen is more efficiently transported to all of the body's systems by the circulation system. This helps the muscles to work more effectively and thereby increases stamina as well as long-term muscle health.

reduced stress Stress reduction is a major benefit of Pilates. Overtension of muscles increases stress, while stretching with breathing enhances levels of relaxation.

improved digestion The stomach and the intestines are muscles. Pilates helps to tone and relax these muscles, bringing them into their optimum state. This in turn improves the digestive processes that go on within them. In addition, because Pilates helps to reduce stress, overproduction of stomach acids becomes less likely, which reduces the risk of ulcers and other stomach problems.

clearer skin As your circulation becomes more efficient, you improve the body's ability to clear toxins. In this way, practicing Pilates can lead to clearer skin.

trimmer waist, flatter stomach and more toned buttocks and thighs The steadily controlled movements in Pilates work the muscles slowly and thoroughly, which leads to better tone. A more efficient muscle burns body fat more quickly, especially around the waist and hips.

stimulates the immune system A stronger, more relaxed body encourages a good immune system. This is because the circulation of lymph (fluid carrying white blood cells) relies on good muscle movement to pump it around the body. Improved circulation will add to the effect.

how does *Pilates* work?

Pilates exercising is known for its ability to redefine the shape of people's bodies, sculpting them into a naturally optimum form. The reason that it does this so well is because it is such an efficient form of physical exercise and works on different levels of the physical body, including the nervous system, the muscular system, the fascia system, and the skeletal system.

There are four major areas of the body on which Pilates actually works. These are:

- The nervous system
- The muscular system
- The fascia system
- The skeletal system.

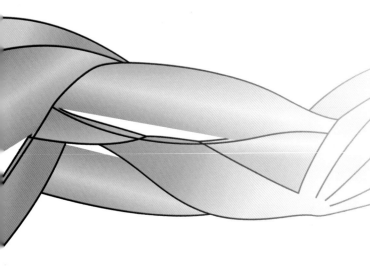

Pilates helps you to retrain your muscular system to move in the most effective way. If your muscles are used to being tense or flaccid, this may take time to achieve. However, the more you bring your muscles back to optimum relaxation, the more comfortable they become in this state.

The nervous system

The nervous system is vital for the control and coordination of movement. It is divided into the central and peripheral systems. The central system includes the brain and spinal cord, while the peripheral system consists of the nerves that course throughout the body. These peripheral nerves deliver messages to the body from the central system and relay messages back from the far reaches of the body. This is how the body "speaks" and provides feedback to the brain. Pilates brings greater awareness of the nervous system and helps you to develop a better sense of how your limbs, muscles, and internal organs feel. In turn, this helps you to find the centered point between tension and relaxation, one of the foundations of Pilates practice.

The muscular system

Not many people are aware that good and effective muscle contraction begins from a state of relaxation. Achieving a state of relaxation before movement produces more power and control. It also means that there is less risk of injury and less pressure on your joints when you move. With a more relaxed and toned muscle system, you are more stable and will burn fat more efficiently. This leads to good body tone, a flatter abdomen, and tighter buttocks.

Muscle contraction begins from three positions:

- Optimum relaxation
- Overcontraction
- Overstretching.

Optimum relaxation

This is what we are trying to achieve in Pilates. Optimum relaxation is where the muscles and tendons rest with a tension that is full and comfortable. You can only burn off fat if your fat burning tissues (muscles) are efficient. Optimum relaxation makes for the most efficient movement. Animals demonstrate this when they run—the movement is relaxed and fluid.

Overcontraction

This is when the muscle, with its tendon, does not let go even when you stop moving. Many people have overcontracted shoulders, for example, which remain tight when they try to relax. An overcontracted muscle pulls the joint toward the side of the contraction. This means that when you move, you are not starting from the neutral position and will suffer a slight loss of power. Continued movement from an overcontracted starting point could increase the wear and tear on a joint. If your back muscles are overcontracted, you increase the risk of injury and your central stability is disturbed.

Overstretching

Overstretched muscles around a joint can lead to serious instability. If the muscle tone is flaccid and weak, reflex reactions will be slow and the risk of injury will be increased. Sudden recurring strains and sprains, especially in the back, knees, and shoulders, are generally due to this type of underlying problem. In addition, an overstretched muscle will not be able to burn fat effectively.

Thousands of nerves run all over the body, carrying messages to and from the brain. Pilates helps you to develop better body awareness. In other words, it helps you to pay more attention to these messages and adjust your position and movements accordingly.

1 Anatomy

Once you have embarked on a regular Pilates routine, you will
become far more aware of the different components of your
body and how they work together. You can always spot an
experienced Pilates practitioner by their impeccable posture!
The secret is a well-aligned skeletal system, with spine,
shoulders and pelvis in their natural, "neutral" position,
supported by strong but flexible muscles. As you increase the
frequency of your ten-minute sessions and your technique
gradually improves, you will begin to find this optimum posture
automatically. It won't be long before your new-found discipline
spills over into everyday life, giving you a physical grace you
never knew before.

anatomy:*bones*

One of the main aims of Pilates is to bring the skeletal system back to its natural alignment. The key points of the skeleton that are involved are the spine, the shoulder girdle, and the pelvis, which are all essential to maintaining good posture. Pilates also mobilizes the joints, and can help increase bone density, reducing the risk of osteoporosis and its associated problems, such as fractures.

The spine

The spine is made up of 34 separate bones, called vertebrae. These form a column to protect the delicate spinal cord, a key part of the nervous system that delivers messages throughout the body from the brain and returns messages from the body to the brain. The spine also connects and supports the rest of the skeleton.

Viewed from behind, the spine appears to be straight from top to bottom, but if you look at it in profile, you will see that it has four natural curves, which act as shock absorbers during movement. A number of the Pilates exercises instruct you to ensure that your spine is in "neutral." This means that you let your spine rest in its natural curves. If you are standing up, you should neither stretch out the spine unnaturally, nor slump so that the curves are exaggerated. When you are lying down, do not press your back down into the floor or arch it so that the lower back comes up off the floor. Simply relax, so that your spine falls into its natural, "neutral" position.

When doing Pilates, you are also often asked to roll or unroll the back, one vertebra at a time. The vertebrae are joined together by ligaments, and cartilage disks between each vertebra prevent friction. This segmented, protected structure enables you to roll and unroll in a controlled, flowing way.

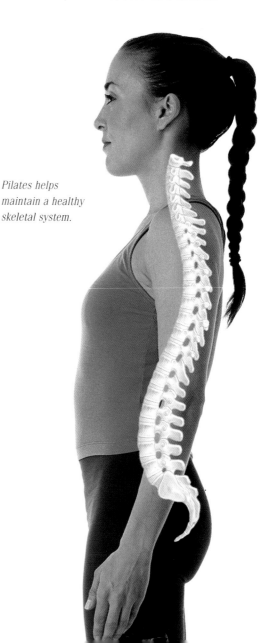

Pilates helps maintain a healthy skeletal system.

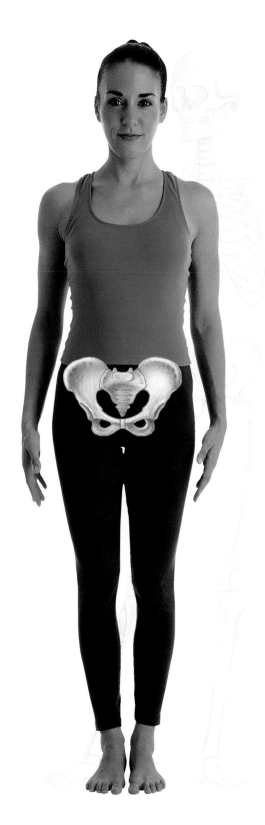

The shoulder girdle

The arms are joined to the torso at the shoulders. Three bones are attached to each shoulder—the clavicle, or collar bone, which is also joined to the top of the breastbone; the scapula, or shoulder blade; and the humerus, or upper arm bone. There is plenty of scope for bad posture stemming from the shoulders. We are often told to "stand up straight," but this may encourage you to pull your shoulders too far back into an unnatural position, causing strain across the collar bone and upper ribcage. You may habitually sit slumped forward, perhaps because your desk and chair are the wrong height, causing strain across the back, or your shoulders may have become unbalanced as a result of carrying heavy shopping. Tension is often carried in the shoulders, causing them to hunch up toward your ears. Finding the correct position for your shoulders is essential to creating good posture and correcting any back pain.

The pelvis

The pelvis is joined to the lower part of the spine, and the legs are attached to the pelvis at the hip joints. A misaligned pelvis is another common problem, which can be caused by an unbalanced sitting position, for example, or by holding a baby propped on a hip. The abdominal muscles, which form part of the central "core," are attached to the pelvis at the pubic bone. Putting the pelvis into "neutral" means neither pushing it back (so that your bottom sticks out and your lower spine curves unnaturally), nor pushing it forward, (so that your stomach sticks out and your spine is straightened). Again, the pelvis should be allowed to fall into its natural, neutral position so that it doesn't cause strain elsewhere.

A correctly aligned pelvis is essential to maintaining good posture.

anatomy: *muscles*

Muscles need to be used frequently to stay strong, and also stretched regularly to stay flexible. Unfortunately, the modern inclination to travel everywhere by car, often coupled with the necessity of spending long hours sitting at a desk, means that many people do not give their muscles the attention they need to stay healthy. By focusing on and controlling each of the main muscle groups, Pilates exercises will enable you to bring your muscles back to peak condition.

When muscles are not used very much, they become weak and lose elasticity, making movement more difficult—if you have ever had an illness that has kept you in bed even for just a few days, you will know how weak and wobbly you feel when you first get up and start to move about again. Pilates recognized that prolonged lack of use, following major illness or serious injury, led to the physical infirmity he suffered as a child, and he was a great believer in starting rehabilitation as early as possible to avoid unnecessary muscle wastage. (If you are recovering from a major illness or injury, you should always consult your doctor and a registered Pilates practitioner to advise you on a program of rehabilitation.)

Muscles are tissues that work together in pairs to create movement—as one muscle contracts, the other relaxes. To help you visualize this in action, hold out your arm in front of you with your hand palm down and fingers pointing forward, parallel to the floor. Now let your hand flop down at the wrist—you can see how the muscles on the upper side of the wrist relax and stretch to let the muscles on the under side of the wrist contract. The more you pull your fingers back toward the under side of your wrist, the more the upper

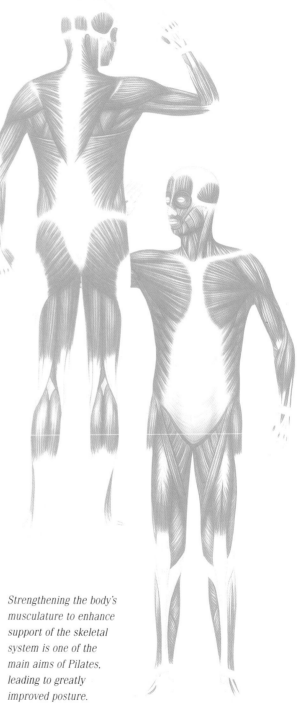

Strengthening the body's musculature to enhance support of the skeletal system is one of the main aims of Pilates, leading to greatly improved posture.

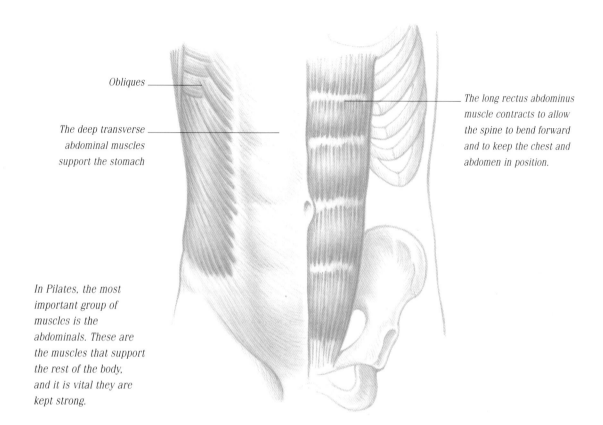

Obliques

The long rectus abdominus muscle contracts to allow the spine to bend forward and to keep the chest and abdomen in position.

The deep transverse abdominal muscles support the stomach

In Pilates, the most important group of muscles is the abdominals. These are the muscles that support the rest of the body, and it is vital they are kept strong.

muscles have to stretch and the tighter the lower muscles become to let the movement take place.

Muscles are at their most powerful and effective when they are well-toned but also relaxed. If your muscles have either become very tense (overcontracted) or are completely lacking in tone (overstretched), any movement can quickly lead to injury. An overcontracted muscle will stay tight even when you are not moving, and movement from an overcontracted muscle can lead to wear and tear on a joint as it tries to compensate by pulling toward the muscle. A weak, overstretched muscle can lead to instability around a joint, resulting in slow reflex actions. The Pilates exercises in this book aim to tone the muscles so that they are strong but flexible, enabling all movement to start from a state of relaxation.

The most important muscles targeted by the Pilates technique are those that form the "girdle of strength"—

primarily the deep postural transversus abdominus and lumbar multifidus, supported by the pelvic floor muscles. If your abdominal muscles are very weak at the outset, you will need to devote some time to strengthening them, or you may find other, stronger muscle groups trying to take over the work. It is very tempting, for example, to engage the gluteus maximus— the buttocks—instead of the pelvic floor muscles, especially as you are more likely to be able to feel the contraction. Similarly, you may find yourself trying to flex the upper body by lifting the head and shoulders and tensing the muscles in the upper back, instead of using your abdominal muscles. However, once you have a sufficiently strong and toned "girdle of strength", you will find that all your movement becomes easier and more fluid. You can then concentrate on working on muscle groups elsewhere, confident that you are supported by a strong center.

Anatomy   15

2   PostureandBodyType

Most of us are far too busy getting on with the business of living to pay much attention to our posture. Yet the way we stand and sit—even the way we lie—has a significant impact on our body's well-being. Bad posture that remains uncorrected can place intolerable strain on other parts of the body, leading to a range of postural distortions and conditions.

Getting the balance right is a central tenet of Pilates. Once you are used to finding and maintaining good posture during your ten-minute sessions, you will soon start reviewing your habitual postures in your daily routine. It won't be long before other people notice the difference as well as you.

By bringing your body back to its aligned state and building up your muscle tone, you will be helping to make the most of what is natural to you. Remember that everyone's natural body shape is in some way unique, and the visible results of your Pilates practice will largely depend on your body type.

posture

Posture is the starting point of all movement. If your posture is under strain, every movement you make will be inefficient, which leads to tiredness, weakness, and aching muscles and joints. This is why you begin every Pilates exercise by adopting a good posture and relaxing into it and also why you need to incorporate good posture into your daily life.

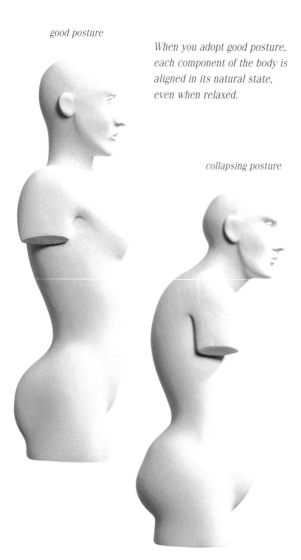

good posture

When you adopt good posture, each component of the body is aligned in its natural state, even when relaxed.

collapsing posture

Posture is the way in which you stand, sit, or lie. You should be able to relax in whatever posture you have adopted and still maintain good muscle tone. If you relax and your posture collapses, then this is an indication that you need to work on your body's stability, for example, by practicing the Pilates exercises.

Good posture

You can check your standing posture quite easily if you stand facing a mirror and scan down your body. The following are signs of good posture:

- Level ear lobes
- Level shoulders
- Equal distance between the ears and shoulders
- Equal spaces between arms and body
- Level hips
- Level left and right kneecaps
- Equal shape and contour in your calf muscles
- Equal arches of the feet.

Let yourself relax. If you feel a strain on your neck, back, hips, or legs, then your posture needs correcting.

Bad posture is common. The strain manifests itself in aches and pains, which can lead to serious health problems.

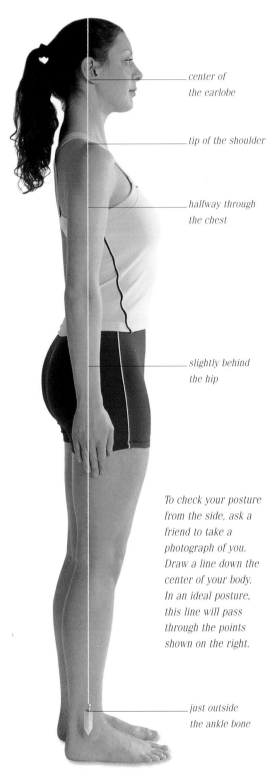

center of
the earlobe

tip of the shoulder

halfway through
the chest

slightly behind
the hip

*To check your posture
from the side, ask a
friend to take a
photograph of you.
Draw a line down the
center of your body.
In an ideal posture,
this line will pass
through the points
shown on the right.*

just outside
the ankle bone

Collapsing posture

It is from the side that distorted posture is classified
into its six major groups. These are:

- Cervical lordosis
- Thoracic kyphosis
- Thoracic straight spine
- Lumbar lordosis
- Swayback
- Visceroptosis.

It is quite common for postures to combine several
different elements of these conditions.

Cervical lordosis

In this posture, the neck spine has moved too far
backward and the vertebrae below it too far forward.
As the back of the head and the upper back get closer
together, the chin points forward. The muscles at the
back of the neck shorten and those at the front become
overstretched and tight. At the same time, the vertebrae
move forward, stretching and weakening the ligaments
at the front of the spine. Joints at the back of the spine
suffer compression, which increases wear and tear.
Arthritis and other forms of joint inflammation may
develop as a result of cervical lordosis, as well as neck
pain and stiffness.

Thoracic kyphosis

In this posture, the upper back gives the impression
that the person is falling forward. As the forward
movement progresses, the muscles at the back of
the spine stretch and weaken, and the muscles at
the front shorten and weaken. Under this pressure,
the vertebrae become distorted, the breastbone drops,
and the chest becomes compressed. This decreases
the efficiency of the lungs and heart. The stomach and
intestines also become compressed, which can lead to
digestion problems.

postural conditions

Together with those described on the previous page, these are the most common postural distortions. It can be helpful to recognize your particular postural condition so that you can bring your attention to areas of concern as you do the exercises. You may also be able to choose techniques that specifically work to realign areas affected by your posture.

Few people maintain perfect posture into their adult lives. Many of us will suffer from one or other of these spinal postural problems or those described on the previous page.

Thoracic straight spine

This is a condition where the thoracic spine becomes straight as a result of the shortening of the muscles on the back of the spine. As they contract, the spine straightens, leading to compression of nerves and a disturbance of the ribs. People who suffer from this condition may feel pain and tingling in the arms. In addition, the chest, heart, and lungs come under pressure, which reduces their efficiency.

Lumbar lordosis

In an exaggerated lumbar lordosis, the vertebrae of the lower back move forward, giving the appearance that the person is falling backward. This increases pressure on the back of the vertebrae, leading to weakness and pain in the lower back. The abdominal muscles weaken and the stomach is dragged forward with the intestines. Digestion is disturbed as the circulation to the digestion tract becomes overstretched.

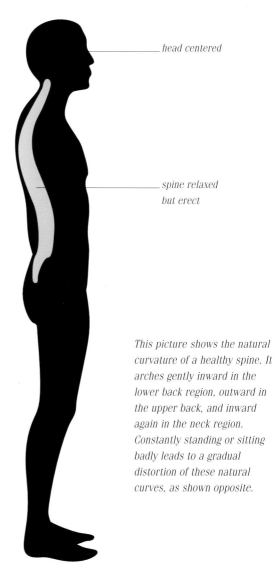

head centered

spine relaxed but erect

This picture shows the natural curvature of a healthy spine. It arches gently inward in the lower back region, outward in the upper back, and inward again in the neck region. Constantly standing or sitting badly leads to a gradual distortion of these natural curves, as shown opposite.

Swayback

The swayback posture is a more overall disturbance than the other postural conditions described. Beginning with a backward tipping of the head, it is a long distortion that begins in the thoracic spine, moving down into the lumbar spine, and creating what seems to be a backward pushing of the knees. This is essentially a weakness of the ligaments in the body. Poor muscle tone adds to the problem and there is generally a poor control of movement. Joints, particularly the elbow, may appear double-jointed.

Visceroptosis

This is the loss of abdominal muscle tone and includes the "beer belly" and bloating on the lower bowel and pelvis. The intestines, kidneys, and womb are dragged downward, overstretching tissues and reducing circulatory and nutritional supply. This precipitates such conditions as period pain, incontinence, and irritable bowel syndrome.

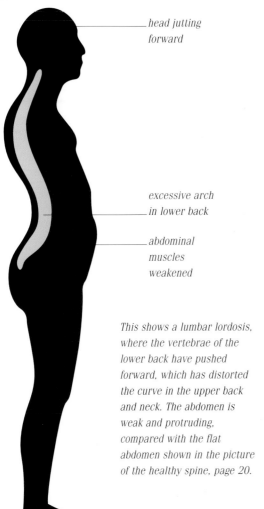

head jutting forward

excessive arch in lower back

abdominal muscles weakened

This shows a lumbar lordosis, where the vertebrae of the lower back have pushed forward, which has distorted the curve in the upper back and neck. The abdomen is weak and protruding, compared with the flat abdomen shown in the picture of the healthy spine, page 20.

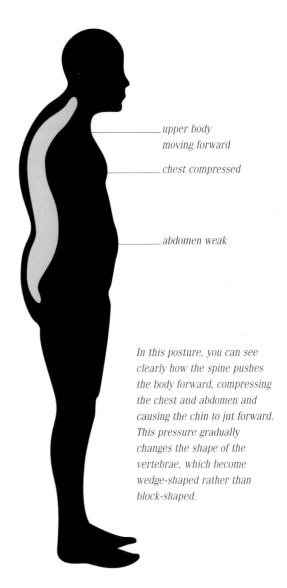

upper body moving forward

chest compressed

abdomen weak

In this posture, you can see clearly how the spine pushes the body forward, compressing the chest and abdomen and causing the chin to jut forward. This pressure gradually changes the shape of the vertebrae, which become wedge-shaped rather than block-shaped.

body type

Many people are attracted to Pilates because of its ability to redefine and tone the body. However, Pilates is all about working within your limitations: it will help you to reach your optimum shape but cannot break the confines of your natural body type.

You may notice that your body starts to change quite rapidly when you begin to practice Pilates—simply learning to hold yourself correctly and relax into good posture can make an immediate difference to the way that you look. Over time, as we have seen, muscle tone improves, promoting weight loss, bones and joints move back into alignment, and overall posture gradually returns to its naturally erect state.

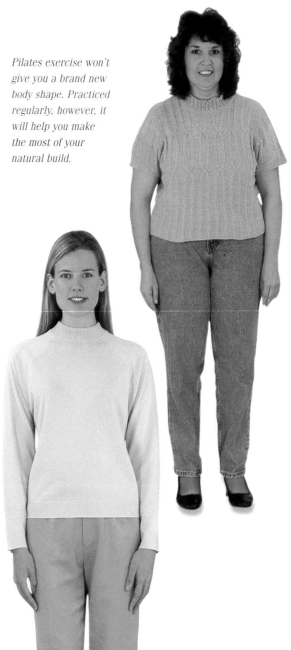

Pilates exercise won't give you a brand new body shape. Practiced regularly, however, it will help you make the most of your natural build.

body types
Our body types are usually defined according to the dominance of our three body cavities. These cavities are the head, chest, and tummy regions. The body is usually categorized into three forms:

- Ectomorph
- Mesomorph
- Endomorph.

These basic body-type descriptions were formulated by the American psychologist William Sheldon. Most of us find ourselves falling between two of these basic types, combining different aspects of both.

The ectomorph is tall and thin with a delicate build and long, thin limbs. Ectomorphs have stooped shoulders and are lightly muscled. They have trouble gaining weight. The mesomorph has a hard, muscular body and is rectangular in overall appearance. Mesomorphs typically have an upright posture, thick skin, and develop muscle quickly. Endomorphs have a generally round shape with underdeveloped muscles and a prominent chest and stomach.

different *body* types

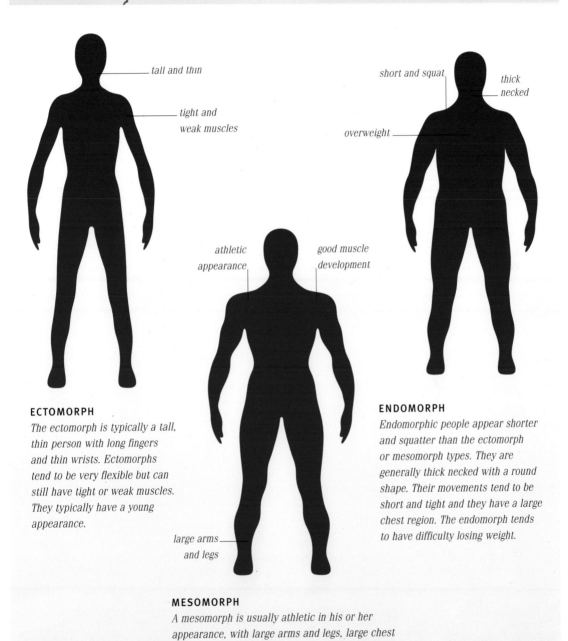

tall and thin

tight and
weak muscles

short and squat

thick
necked

overweight

athletic
appearance

good muscle
development

large arms
and legs

ECTOMORPH
The ectomorph is typically a tall,
thin person with long fingers
and thin wrists. Ectomorphs
tend to be very flexible but can
still have tight or weak muscles.
They typically have a young
appearance.

ENDOMORPH
Endomorphic people appear shorter
and squatter than the ectomorph
or mesomorph types. They are
generally thick necked with a round
shape. Their movements tend to be
short and tight and they have a large
chest region. The endomorph tends
to have difficulty losing weight.

MESOMORPH
A mesomorph is usually athletic in his or her
appearance, with large arms and legs, large chest
and a tight tummy region. Mesomorphs have good
muscle development and are often good at sport.

3 TheBasics

To ensure you make the most of your Pilates practice, you will need to master some core techniques, as set out over the following pages. The time you take perfecting these now will prove invaluable later on.

One of the most important building blocks to successful technique is breathing. Breathing properly, with full control, will give you the necessary focus of mind to concentrate on the different components of your body while you exercise. As you learn to listen to your physical self more closely, all the time visualizing a healthier more balanced you, mind and body will start to fall in step with each other.

Pilates taught that the center of our physical being lies in the abdomen. His technique teaches us to zone in on these muscles, to strengthen and control them. Once you have built a core of stability in this way, you will be able to connect with it regularly, using it as your basis for perfect posture.

vital *techniques*

"Quality of life cannot be achieved by taking the right shortcut. There is no shortcut, but there is a path. The path is based on principles revered throughout history. If there is one message to glean from this wisdom, it is that a meaningful life is not a matter of speed or efficiency. It's much more a matter of what you do and why you do it, than how fast you get it done."

STEPHEN R. COVEY, *First Things*

Mastering the basic techniques of Pilates before you start will ensure that you get maximum benefit from your practice sessions.

When Stephen Covey wrote this passage, he was talking about the organization and management of time—but his principles are appropriate to many things in life, including practice of the Pilates system. Pilates is a path toward a healthy body that functions at maximum efficiency. If you follow the path at the prescribed speed, adhering to the principles and techniques involved, you will get the result you want. If you try to stray from the path, hoping for a quicker result, you are likely to fail. So be patient, stick to your regular ten-minute routines, and learn to enjoy your steady progress. It may seem an uphill task at first, but it will be worth it!

There are many different exercises in this book, ranging from warm-up exercises and beginners' exercises to advanced-level exercises; but the basic principles and techniques of Pilates are common to all, and are vital to the success of the exercises. To begin with, take a little time to read through the following pages, and practice the exercises for breathing and abdominal hollowing—do not attempt to start practicing the Pilates movements, even at the simple warm-up level, until you are confident that you have mastered these basic techniques.

Breathing

Breathing is something we do naturally and instinctively, without thinking, and we take it for granted that the way we breathe is the right way. Very often, however, our

26   Ten-Minute Pilates

breathing is shallow, and we fail to take in sufficient air to oxygenate the blood properly. This in turn leaves us feeling tired and lethargic, adversely affecting both our energy levels and our spirits.

Controlled and effective breathing is vital to the Pilates technique, and mastering the art of breathing correctly is perhaps the steepest of the Pilates learning curves. Disciplines such as martial arts, tai chi, and yoga emphasize the importance of conscious breathing to help calm and focus the mind, release physical tension, and enhance learning—and Pilates is no exception in this approach.

To check whether you breathe properly, lie down on the floor, breathe in through your nose, and observe where that breath is going. If all that happens is that your upper chest moves a little, and then you exhale, your breathing is not effective. If you observe that you take a deep breath, pulling in your stomach tightly, then exhale and let everything go, your breathing is still not effective—in either of these cases, you will need to re-educate yourself.

The Pilates breath is wide and full into your back and sides, filling the lungs like bellows, expanding the diaphragm and pushing your ribcage out to the sides— imagine a pail handle being lifted out. When you exhale, the diaphragm contracts, pushing all the stale air out of the lungs. Each step in the Pilates exercises begins with a direction to inhale or exhale, and the movement accompanies the breath. You must have proper control over your breathing, so that the breath comes and goes in a steady, rhythmic, flowing way—otherwise, you will very likely find yourself holding your breath as you rush through the movement and end up collapsing in a breathless heap!

We wouldn't be human if we didn't take breathing for granted. Yet learning how to breathe properly is one of the most challenging aspects of Pilates, and one of the most important.

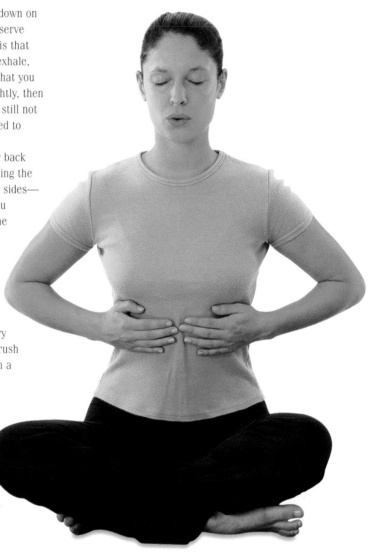

vital *techniques*

Centering

All movement comes from a strong, central "core"—the area below the base of the ribcage and above the line across the hip-bones. Here, the transversus abdominus and the lumbar multifidus muscles form an invisible "girdle of strength" around the body, which Pilates referred to as the "powerhouse." If you have poor posture or a bad back, your center is weak. The first aim of Pilates exercises is to strengthen this area by conditioning and toning the muscles to promote easy, flowing movement and good posture.

Control and concentration

Mental and physical fitness is the result of a constant exchange of information and feedback between mind and body. While you are training, be focused on what you are doing—still your mind and let it listen to your body, and be aware of all sensations. Concentrate fully on each move so that you bring mind and body together to create a pattern of balanced and controlled movements, each one flowing slowly, gently, and gracefully into the next.

Precision

"The benefits of Pilates depend solely on your performing the exercises exactly according to the instructions."
J.H. Pilates

Don't be tempted to do your own thing. Read the directions carefully for each movement, and make sure you understand them before practicing the move. Carry out each move with precision—focus your attention on the relevant area of the body, make sure you are breathing fully and deeply, and inhale and exhale at the correct point in the exercise.

Rushing through each movement and increasing the number of repetitions will not make it more effective—in Pilates, quality is far more important than quantity.

Ten minutes spent doing the exercises correctly, following the instructions to the letter, is worth considerably more than an hour doing your own thing.

Relaxation and alignment

Before starting your Pilates session, take a few minutes to relax your mind and body. It's important that your body is correctly aligned to enable you to carry out the movements in a natural, flowing way with ease and precision. Before you start any movement—whether you are standing, sitting, or lying face up or down—make sure that:

• Your head is in alignment with your body and not tilted to one side or the other.
• Your shoulders are in line with your hips—imagine that your shoulder blades are sliding or "melting" down your back.
• Your knees are in line with your hips.
• Your feet are in line with your knees.
• Your back and pelvis (see pages 18–19) are in "neutral."

Motivation and visualization

Adopting and maintaining a positive mental attitude are key elements in the success of any new venture. Although following a Pilates exercise routine won't take up much of your time from day-to-day, and although you know it will be of benefit to you, it's all too easy to give up before you even start. Phrases such as, "I can't do that; I don't have ten minutes to spare," or "It's too late to change now," are unhelpful—so just don't use them! Instead, say firmly to yourself, "Yes, I can easily find ten minutes and I will succeed." Say it every day! You may feel silly at first, but you'll appreciate it when the results of your efforts start to become visible to you. Before you start practicing the Pilates technique, fix a clear picture in your mind of what you want to achieve. It may be that you simply want to look and feel your best—long, lean, graceful, and brimming with self-confidence—or you may have physical problems that you wish to overcome, such as a bad back. Either way, Pilates is there to help you—as long as you let it.

Now's the time to make a commitment to yourself and your body: draw up a practice schedule and stick to it.

breathing

We have already seen that correct and effective breathing is essential to practicing Pilates—so take some time to learn the breathing technique. You are aiming for a gentle, non-exaggerated breath, and to breathe laterally, encouraging the ribcage to move out to the sides and back. The movement of the ribcage is described as "pail handle"—as you inhale, the ribs move up and out, as if a pail handle were being lifted, and as you exhale, the ribs move back to the center and slightly down, as if the pail handle were being replaced.

3 Close your eyes and for a moment inhale and exhale, as you would normally. Gently press your hands against your body, and feel the movement of your body as you breathe. You may feel your chest rise a little, and your stomach move in and out, or you may feel nothing at all.

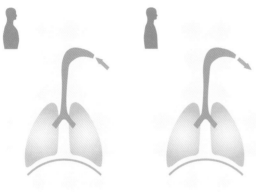

If you are breathing correctly, the chest and diaphragm should expand as you inhale, filling the lungs, and contract as you exhale, pushing the air out of the body.

1 Find a warm, comfortable space and sit down on the floor. You might find it more comfortable with a cushion or a mat.

2 Sit upright, making sure that your shoulders are relaxed and with your legs crossed. Place one hand on your chest and another on your stomach, around the navel area.

4 Now change your hand position. Close together the fingers and thumb of both hands, as if you were going to make a chopping movement. Place the heel of each hand on the side of the ribcage, with the fingers extended to the soft opening at the center. Relax your shoulders and let the shoulder blades melt down your back.

5 Making sure there is no tension in the body, inhale through the nose and exhale with a sigh through a relaxed open jaw: remember the "H" sound in "hollow." Breathe in an even rhythm—try inhaling to a mental count of four and exhaling to a mental count of four. Maintain the relaxed position of your shoulders.

6 Now close your eyes, and sense within your body how you are feeling. You should be sitting comfortably, with your hands apart on the ribcage, shoulders relaxed and the breathing flowing to a gentle rhythm.

7 With the heels of your hands, apply gentle pressure to the ribcage—make your mind and body aware of the area. Inhale gently as if breathing to the heels of your hands, feeling your ribcage expand to the sides; as you exhale, feel the ribs closing into the center. Repeat for nine more breaths. Get a sense of the flow—feel the "pail handle" move out and up, in and down.

Variations

Try the same technique standing up, lying on your back or face down, or in the crook position (sitting up with your knees bent at 45 degrees, feet flat on the floor). It will be easier to find the connection in some positions than in others, but you should try them all in preparation for carrying out the exercises.

body placement and *muscle synergy*

Pilates is a synergistic activity, which means that for each individual movement in each exercise—whatever level you are working at—every part of the body is working together to bring about the desired result. To practice Pilates successfully, it is essential that you identify the core muscle groups, experience them working together, and learn how to control them.

Core conditioning

As we have already discussed, the first priority with Pilates is to create the strong, stable "center" or "core"—which Pilates referred to as the dynamic "girdle of strength" or "powerhouse"—from which stems perfect posture as well as all movement in the body.

When you are practicing the Pilates technique, you will frequently come across the direction to "maintain the connection with the center," and until you can do this with complete ease and without effort, you will not be able to focus all your attention on the area you are working. So what is this all-important center, and where do you find it?

Well, loosely speaking it is the area located between an imaginary line running around the body just below the diaphragm and another running above the pelvic floor. It is three muscles found within this area that are engaged to create a strong center. These are the muscles that stabilize the lower spine in the lumbar region of the back, and they are positioned very deep and close to the spine itself—the transversus abdominus to the front of the spine and the lumbar multifidus to the back, both in line with the navel, and the pelvic floor muscles at the base.

The transversus abdominus is one of the four muscles that make up the abdominal wall, and is the deepest of the four. To help you locate the position of this muscle, stand up so that you are straight but relaxed, take both hands and grab your sides

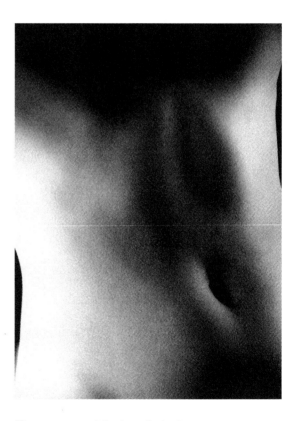

The transversus abdominus, the lumbar multifidus and the pelvic floor are the three groups of muscles that form the "center" in Pilates technique.

with your fingers pointing in toward the navel. When you have a firm hold, give a good cough! As you cough, you will feel a muscle bounce beneath your fingers. Now take a breath in, and then blow out—you will feel the same muscle bounce again. This is the transversus abdominus (TVA) and, because it is such a vital component in core stability, it is essential to learn how to engage it properly.

TVA activation

As with everything, there is a right way and a wrong way to go about activating the TVA. Let's start with the wrong way, which is simply to overdo it by sucking in your abdomen with such gusto that it's almost sticking to your spine. What you are aiming for is to master a gentle contraction of the TVA—one that you can maintain easily at all times, whether you are standing still, walking, or exercising or sitting and either working at a desk or relaxing in your favorite comfortable chair.

To understand the reason for this, you need to know that there are two types of muscle—mobilizers (task muscles) and stabilizers (postural muscles). Muscles that mobilize are responsible for large movements, such as kicking or throwing—they mobilize limbs. Compared to stabilizers, they are superficial (closer to the surface), longer, work harder (at approximately 40–100% of their power) and are phasic—i.e., they tire quickly, so work in phases for short periods, turning on and off.

Muscles that stabilize are close to the spine or lie deeply; they are shorter than mobilizers, work for longer periods, and are tonic (i.e., they hold tone). Stabilizers need endurance and so they work at only about 20–30% of their maximum voluntary contraction (MVC). The TVA is a stabilizer muscle—a deep, postural muscle—so this is why it is important to work it gently.

Before practicing the Pilates technique, you need to learn how to locate and correctly activate the transversus abdominus muscle.

body placement and muscle synergy

Working the TVA

How do you recognize when you are working at the correct level of TVA contraction—30%? Read this exercise through, then try it out.

Stand up, keeping good posture in mind—stand tall, with your knees slightly kinked, but not locked, your tail bone pointing toward the floor, and your shoulders relaxed, as though your shoulder blades were melting down your back towards your pelvis. Hold your head upright, so that your ears point toward the ceiling, and focus your eyes on the horizon. In this position, you will feel elongated—stretched from head to toe. Now let your stomach relax as far as it will go—and give this position a score of 0%. Return to the first position.

Now pull everything in so that your whole body feels sucked in and tense—pull your stomach into your spine and elevate your shoulders until they are almost touching your ears. You should now bear a strong resemblance to Frankenstein! Give this position a score of 100%, so the yardstick is 0% for no tone and 100% for tense to the point of being unable to breathe.

To get to 30%, return to the first position again, standing tall but relaxed. Take your right hand and place your thumb at the lower edge of your navel, then splay your fingers and span your hand until the little finger is toward the pubic bone, resting your hand on your stomach. Draw your navel in and up toward your spine, away from your hand, to 100%, then release it halfway to 50% while retaining your elongated stance—do not slump. Now release a little farther, and you have reached 30%—you should have a sensation of feeling connected but not tense, in a position that you can maintain all day and every day, whatever you are doing.

Follow the exercise (left) to establish what the correct level of TVA contraction feels like. You should aim to maintain this level of tenseness at all times.

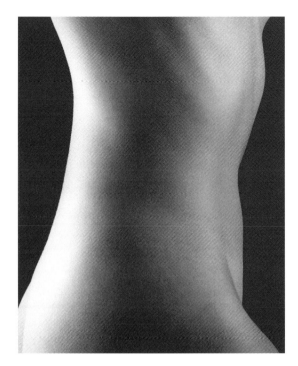

Engaging the pelvic floor

The pelvic floor muscles are an important element in stabilizing the spine, working in conjunction with the TVA. A gentle contraction is sufficient to activate the pelvic floor—do not be tempted to clench the buttocks in an effort to feel the tension. Lie on your back and place your hand on the lower abdominal area, then gently exhale, and draw up the muscles from below and in front of the pelvic area—as you do so, you will feel the TVA contracting.

Neutral pelvis

The pelvis is the base of support for the body—your spine rests upon it and your legs move from it, so for optimum movement the pelvis should be "organized" in the best possible postural position. This position is described as "neutral."

To help you identify the perfect position, lie on your back with your knees bent to 45 degrees, your feet flat on the floor, and your body relaxed. Place your hands in a triangle over your stomach, with your thumbs forming the base of the triangle at the navel, and your fingers splaying toward the pubic bone to form the point. When the pelvis is properly organized, your palms should be flat on your lower stomach muscles, and your hip-bones should be positioned evenly on either side of your hands. If your fingers are raised higher than your thumbs, your pelvis is in a posterior tilt, and if your thumbs are higher than your fingers, it is because your pelvis is in an anterior tilt. When your pelvis is in neutral, your hands will be absolutely level, with your spine neither too flat to the floor nor arched to the ceiling. Practicing the "Neutral to Imprinted Spine (50/50)" exercise on page 65 helps you to settle into this position.

When your pelvis is in the correct, "neutral" position, your hands will be absolutely level in this position.

body placement
and *muscle synergy*

Abdominal hollowing

Abdominal hollowing is created when the deep postural abdominal muscles are contracted, and is the result of correct breathing. As we have already seen, it is essential to inhale and exhale gently, and not try to force the breath. As you inhale, you should get a sense of the ribs moving to the sides and the back, not up and away. As you exhale, drawing the navel in and up toward the spine, you should get a sense of the ribs closing in and moving toward the hips as if on railroad tracks. If you force the breath out, you will engage the external oblique muscles and end up with a bulging, dome-shaped abdomen—not what you want at all!

Practice with the following exercise:

1 Stand or sit comfortably and elongate the spine, lengthening through the crown of your head to the ceiling, and through your tail bone to the floor.

2 Shrug your shoulders to your ears, then roll them gently backward, letting your shoulder blades glide down your back toward your pelvis.

3 With your shoulders relaxed, place one hand on either side of your ribcage, with your fingertips facing each other at the opening between the ribcage. Inhale gently, and feel your ribcage moving gently out toward the sides as you do so.

4 Exhale gently, relaxing the jaw and sighing softly through an open mouth. Draw up on the pelvic floor and back on the navel toward the spine to a maximum of 30%, as described earlier, feeling the ribs move in toward the center and gently downward, creating the hollow—a "slope" from the ribs to the pelvis. If you exhale to the "H" sound of "hollow," it will open the mouth and drop the jaw, helping you resist the temptation to either blow out or force the exhale through pursed lips.

Lengthening the neck

All Pilates movements are geared toward realigning the body into a perfect posture, with the spine in optimum alignment. The neck—the top of the spine, or "cervical spine"—is a very important part of this process. Maintaining correct alignment in the neck is particularly important when you are flexing the upper body off the floor. It's tempting to lift with the shoulders and head, jamming the chin into the chest or, even worse, hanging the head backward like a hinged coffeepot lid.

To lengthen the neck in preparation for flexing the upper body correctly from a strong central core, rock the chin SLIGHTLY toward the chest, without lifting your head—you should feel as if someone has taken your head in both hands and gently stretched it away from your shoulders. Your neck will now remain in alignment.

The gaze

When you walk along gazing at the floor, your head is downcast and your posture slumped forward—but look up and focus your gaze on the horizon, and you will stand tall and upright, with your head and neck in alignment with your spine. Perfect!

Directing your gaze at the horizon when you are carrying out the Pilates movements will help the movement flow as well as helping you maintain alignment. If you are doing a sit-up, for example, and you keep your gaze on the ceiling, your head will fall back, compressing your neck and spine. If you let your gaze follow the horizon as you move, however, so that it is focused in front of you at knee level when you reach the top of the movement, your head and neck will be aligned and in the optimum position. This is a good example of the synergistic nature of Pilates—you will find it progressively easier to direct your gaze correctly as your center becomes stronger and more stable. Your center will become stronger when you let it do its work and do not inadvertently substitute other muscle groups by directing your gaze incorrectly.

visualization and feedback

Pilates is as much about the mind as it is the body. By discovering the techniques and maintaining regular practice, you will be helping to build a bridge between the mental side of your being and the physical. Once you become aware of all your body is doing for you and all it is capable of, you will value it all the more.

Most of us practice visualization techniques regularly without realizing it. Use your skills to imagine a brand new you.

Visualization

"When we create something, we always create it first in a thought form. A thought or idea always precedes manifestation ... Imagination is the ability to create an idea or mental picture in your mind. In creative visualization, you use your imagination to create a clear image of something to manifest. Then you continue to focus on the idea."

SHAKTI GAWAIN, *Creative Visualisation*

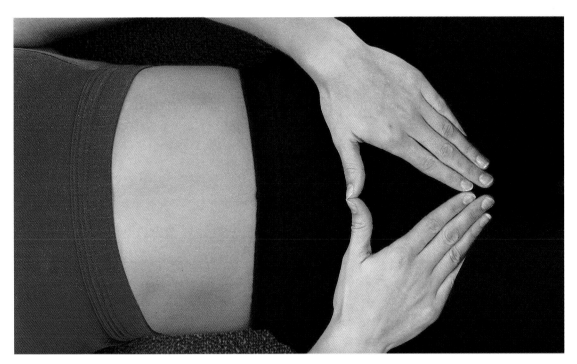

To visualize something is to create a picture of the desired outcome in your mind's eye and to hold it there as a constant source of inspiration and motivation. If this sounds unrealistic to you, think about how often you visualize things without realizing that this is what you are doing. For instance, you take a look around your living-room, which is looking a bit old and tired. You hate that flowery wallpaper, and would love to replace it with plain painted walls. Two new sofas would look great instead of the old-fashioned suite. That clutter needs sorting, and the things you want to keep could be stored away neatly instead of piling up in the corners. Some new drapes and a huge vase of fresh flowers instead of that dusty, withered old houseplant would complete the look. You see? You've created a clear image in your mind of a change you would like to make! You will probably continue to focus on the idea until your revamped living-room is completed.

Why not try the same technique on yourself, and visualize a new you? Take a look at the jaded old you, with all your aches and pains and stresses reflected in your face and posture. Now visualize the new you—upright and confident, sleek and streamlined, free from stress and ailments, glowing with health and vitality. Sounds good? Well, it worked for Joseph Pilates and it

Imagine you have a glass of water that is balanced on the triangle formed by your hands. Try to draw your navel gently back toward your spine—without spilling a drop!

can work for you. Just hold the image in your mind, and focus on it as you are working with Pilates technique. You can keep your goal in mind by hanging your favorite—but perhaps, at the moment, rather too tight?—outfit where you can see it as you exercise, and visualize yourself fitting into it and looking better than ever before. Or try taking a photograph before you start, then take more at regular intervals so that you can see how well you have progressed—a visual source of motivation and measure of achievement!

Biofeedback and body awareness

Biofeedback is a tool that will assist the mind–body connection. Most of us move around on automatic pilot, unaware of how it should feel to connect or contract a muscle correctly.

4 BeforeYouStart

One of the most important lessons your Pilates training will teach

you is to know your own body and what it is capable of. There's

no sense in starting your practice session if you are suffering

from flu, for example, or if you are so cold you risk injury. Plan

your sessions well: set aside a space in the home that you can

quickly and simply set up as an exercise environment. Take your

ten minutes slowly and work with your body, not against it.

preparation

Self-help books like this one mean that you can take control of your own fitness and decide when and where to exercise. However, you don't have a teacher to help you make sure that you practice carefully, so you will need to take full responsibility for your own safety.

Although you are only planning relatively short, ten-minute sessions of Pilates, in your own home, it's important to think about the following aspects of your health and situation before you start:
- Practice environment
- Present age and general state of health
- Pregnancy
- Minor illnesses
- Good practice.

The environment

The immediate environment is often overlooked as a factor that can promote or retard the effectiveness of any exercise system. It is particularly important that you are in a warm area so you don't get cold and tense up your body. However, do not practice in direct sunlight, either outside or in front of a window, or close to a radiator or electric fire, which will heat your body up artificially. In addition, make sure that your practice area has good ventilation and is free from any drafts.

You don't need any special equipment to do Pilates at home, but make sure that you practice in a clear, comfortable space. Lie on a rug, carpet, or folded towel to help keep yourself warm.

Present age and health

With regards to your present age and health, it is important to take advice from a medical professional or qualified Pilates trainer before practicing if you answer "yes" to any of the following questions:

• Are you very young or old? Generally, Pilates is safe for people of all ages, but it is safer to check if you are at either end of the spectrum.
• Do you have diabetes?
• Do you have a history of heart or lung conditions?
• Are you on any medication that could put you at risk while exercising?
• If you are postmenopausal, do you have aches or pains that could indicate lack of bone density?
• Do you have any inflammations or swelling in muscles and/or joints?
• Do you have any disease or injury that makes your muscles and/or joints unstable? These include arthritis, torn ligaments, or dislocations.
• Are your periods accompanied by severe pain? You may be at risk when you are menstruating. In general, you should not practice Pilates if you are suffering from any severe menstrual symptoms, such as back pain, headaches, or weakness. None of these conditions is an absolute disqualifying factor; it may simply mean that you need to avoid doing certain exercises that might aggravate the ailment.

Pregnancy

Pregnancy is not an illness. As long as you feel well, can still move around easily, and the bump is not in the way, there is no reason to stop practicing, or even not take up, Pilates when you are pregnant. If you have any doubts, seek medical advice before you start.

Minor illnesses

Do not attempt to work off any minor illness with Pilates. This is especially important in cases of viral chest, throat, influenza, and glandular infections, which affect your muscular system. Make sure you have been free from these for at least two weeks.

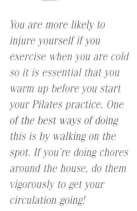

You are more likely to injure yourself if you exercise when you are cold so it is essential that you warm up before you start your Pilates practice. One of the best ways of doing this is by walking on the spot. If you're doing chores around the house, do them vigorously to get your circulation going!

practicing *safely*

Take a few moments to check how you are feeling before, during, and after practicing Pilates. This will help to make sure that you meet your body's needs and that your exercise program is both effective and safe. It will also help to increase your general body awareness, which is an important part of the Pilates approach. Do not force your body past its capabilities.

Pilates is intended to improve your physical and mental well-being, so it is important to make sure that you feel good while you are practicing and that you support your well-being before and after practice. As you develop your practice, you may find that you naturally begin to incorporate better body awareness and activity into your everyday life.

Drinking enough water is an essential part of healthy living as water helps the body to clear out toxins. Try to drink at least two liters of water every day.

Good practice

Safe practice can be divided into:
• Pre-practice preparation and daily activity
• Practice
• Post-practice.

Pre-practice

• In general, you should make sure that you are well hydrated—drink at least nine cups of water a day slowly. However, don't drink a large quantity of liquid just before your Pilates session.
• Do not start your practice session if you are in a state of tension. If you are feeling stressed, try walking on the spot to release tension in your body before you begin the session.
• If you are cold, move gently on the spot to warm up.
• Do not warm up artificially before exercise, for example by sitting in a hot bath, having a shower, or sitting in front of a heater. This can increase the potential for injury.
• Clear your practice area and make sure that you have enough space to stretch out fully during the exercises without knocking into anything.
• Make sure the floor surface is warm—use a mat, rug, or folded towel to practice on.

Post-practice

• Do not just sit down or stop moving after you finish your exercise session. Move into some gentle activity, such as taking a shower and getting dressed.
• Do not go straight to bed after going through your exercises in the evening.

Don't let the brevity of your exercise session fool you into rushing it. Respect your body and don't try to do too much too quickly.

Practice

• Take your ten minutes slowly and carefully. Control the speed at which you exercise and the number of exercises you do in one session.
• Remember, there will be a gentle increase in the strain on your system over your practice time. For these changes to be beneficial, you must not push yourself too hard.
• Some exercises will seem very gentle while you are doing them and you may not feel their effects until a day or two later. Give yourself a week before returning to exercises like these. This will allow the right body adaptation to take place.

Going for a short walk after a Pilates session—perhaps to the shops or the bus stop—will help you to manage a smooth transition back to your normal activity. Enjoy your enhanced body awareness and notice if you are holding yourself slightly differently.

5 WarmingUp

The warm-up exercises on the following pages will help you release any tension held in the mind or body before you start your Pilates session. If you are completely new to the Pilates system, limit your ten minutes to the warm-up exercises only, just for a week or two, while you start to put into practice the techniques and principles you learned in the previous section.

At first, repeat each warm-up movement only three to five times (on each side of the body, where relevant). As you become familiar with the moves, increase the number of repetitions—adding an extra one at each session—to a maximum of ten. Relax, concentrate, and work slowly and steadily, following the directions precisely. Do not try to push any of the moves too far, too soon—you are making progress the whole time, even if it does not seem that way. You may find that this stage is enough of a challenge in itself at first, but in no time at all you will have loosened up your joints and started to improve your muscle tone.

focus on breath

AIM: *To focus your attention on your posture and breathing.*

BENEFITS: *The mind and the whole body.*

1 Stand upright with your shoulders and spine in neutral. Place your feet hip-width apart, keep your knees soft, and let your arms hang loosely.

2 Close your eyes and focus on your breathing. Inhale through your nose, and visualize clean, energizing air entering your body and filling your lungs.

3 Exhale, expelling all the stale air from your system. Continue breathing in this way, making sure your body stays relaxed.

At first, inhale and exhale like this five times, increasing to a maximum of ten.

shrugs

AIM: *To release tension from the neck and shoulders.*

BENEFITS: *Shoulders, neck, and upper body.*

1 Stand upright with your shoulder girdle and spine in neutral. Place your feet hip-width apart, keep your knees soft, and let your arms hang loosely. Focus on your breathing

2 Inhale, and lift your shoulders up toward your ears.

3 Exhale, and draw the shoulder blades into neutral. At first, do the shrugs five times, increasing to a maximum of ten.

rolling down

Aim: *To mobilize the spine and connect with the center.*

Benefits: *The spine, shoulders, and upper body.*

1 Stand upright with your shoulder girdle and spine in neutral. Place your feet hip-width apart, keep your knees soft, and let your arms hang loosely by your sides. Close your eyes and focus your attention on your breathing.

2 Inhale, and lengthen through the spine.

3 Exhale, engaging the pelvic floor muscles and TVA, navel to spine at 30%. Gently nod your chin toward your chest, then roll forward, keeping the ribcage soft and rolling toward the hips. Sense each vertebra rolling, one at a time.

4 Only roll down to your point of comfort—do not try to go too far too soon. At the bottom of the move, inhale, feeling the air inflate your spine and keeping the pelvic floor muscles and abdominals engaged.

5 Roll back up, one vertebra at a time. As you finish the roll, exhale and release the shoulder blades to neutral. At first, do the roll five times, increasing to a maximum of ten.

head turns

AIM: *To release tension from the neck.*

BENEFITS: *The neck and shoulders.*

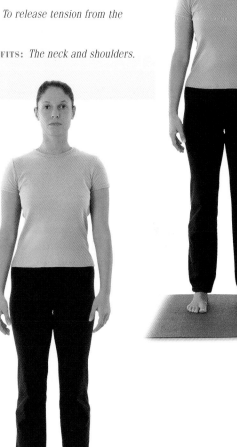

1 Stand upright with your shoulder girdle and spine in neutral. Place your feet hip-width apart, keep your knees soft, and let your arms hang loosely by your sides.

2 Inhale, to prepare.

3 Exhale, engaging the pelvic floor muscles and TVA, navel to spine at 30%. Turn your head to look over your right shoulder, keeping your head in line with your gaze on the horizon.

4 Inhale, and return to center. Repeat the movement five times in this direction.

5 Repeat the movement five times in the opposite direction.

pivot

AIM: *To mobilize the whole body and promote coordination.*

BENEFITS: *The spine, shoulders, hips, arms, and legs.*

1 Stand upright with your shoulder girdle and spine in neutral. Place your feet wider than hip-width apart, keep your knees soft, and let your arms hang loosely by your sides. Inhale, engaging the pelvic floor muscles and TVA, navel to spine at 30%. Lengthen through the spine.

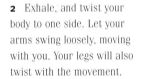

2 Exhale, and twist your body to one side. Let your arms swing loosely, moving with you. Your legs will also twist with the movement.

3 Inhale, and twist back to the center.

4 Exhale, and twist to the other side.

5 Inhale, and twist back to the center.

6 Each time you twist, raise your arms higher, until they reach over your head, then work them back down to your sides, in a continuous, flowing movement. Take three twists in each direction to get to the top of the movement, and three more twists in each direction to get back down.

shell stretch

progression

Aim: *To stretch and lengthen the spine.*

Benefits: *The spine, shoulders, neck, and abdomen.*

Once you are at ease with this movement, you can increase the intensity of the stretch.

Starting from Step 3, ease your buttocks off your heels and "walk" your hands a farther 6–8 inches. With both palms down flat and your head between your elbows, ease your buttocks back toward your heels. This time the stretch will also be felt in your upper back and shoulders.

1 Kneel on all fours, with your knees under your hips and your arms in line with your shoulders, with the elbows soft but not locked. Drop your head between your arms.

2 Inhale, to prepare.

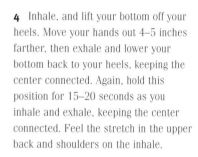

4 Inhale, and lift your bottom off your heels. Move your hands out 4–5 inches farther, then exhale and lower your bottom back to your heels, keeping the center connected. Again, hold this position for 15–20 seconds as you inhale and exhale, keeping the center connected. Feel the stretch in the upper back and shoulders on the inhale.

5 Exhale, and relax.

3 Exhale, engaging the pelvic floor muscles and TVA, navel to spine at 30%. Lower your bottom to your heels, keeping your hands on the floor in front of you and your head resting between your elbows. Hold this position for 15–20 seconds as you inhale and exhale, keeping the center connected. Feel the spine lengthen on the inhale.

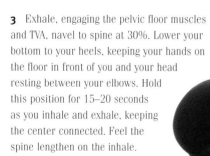

cat stretch

AIM: *To mobilize the spine and help with stabilization.*

BENEFITS: *The spine, shoulders, neck, and abdomen.*

3 Exhale, engaging the pelvic floor and pulling your navel back to your spine. Keep the abdominals scooped to the spine for support. Flex the spine, curling from the end of the tail bone up toward the head.

1 Kneel on all fours, with your spine and shoulder girdle in neutral, your knees under your hips and your hands under your shoulders. Keep your elbows slightly kinked, but not locked.

2 Inhale, keeping your body in neutral.

4 Inhale, at the top of the movement.

5 Exhale, and lengthen through the spine to the start position, keeping the spine in neutral.

6 Inhale, to prepare.

7 Exhale, and repeat the movement. Start with five repetitions and increase to a maximum of ten.

mermaid (side bend)

AIM: *To stretch and flex the spine, with the core connected.*

BENEFITS: *The shoulders, neck, spine, and abdominals.*

1 Stand upright with your shoulder girdle and spine in neutral. Place your feet hip-width apart, keep your knees soft, and let your arms hang loosely by your sides.

2 Standing tall and relaxed, inhale and take the left arm above your head, with the fingers pointing to the sky. Stretch through your fingers, keeping the arm strong.

3 Exhale, and side bend to the right, keeping your pelvis in neutral. Let your head and arm follow your spine.

5 Exhale, and let your arm flow back down by your side. Slide your shoulder blades back into neutral, making sure there is no tension in the head, neck, and shoulder complex.

6 Repeat the movement to the left. Do a total of five side bends on each side.

4 Inhale, and float back up to center, keeping your arm extended.

c-curve

Aim: *To mobilize the spine and strengthen the central core.*

Benefits: *The spine, neck, shoulders, and abdominals.*

1 Sit on the floor, with your knees bent, your weight evenly distributed over both sitting bones and your spine in neutral.

2 Place your hands lightly behind your knees. This will give you support and feedback, but do not pull on your hands as you carry out the move. Relax your shoulders, with the shoulder blades melting down your back. Inhale, and sense the inflation, elongating through the spine.

3 Exhale, engaging the pelvic floor muscles and TVA, navel to spine at 30%. Rock back off the pelvis toward the floor.

modification

Relax your feet and lift your toes, resting only your heels on the floor. This will take the tension out of your hip flexors and so release the muscles.

4 Pause, inhale and return to the upright start position. Keep the abdominals scooped and hollowed throughout the whole move for support. Only go as far as you can each time without shuddering or lifting your feet off the floor. Repeat the movement five times, increasing to a maximum of ten.

trunk rotation

AIM: *To strengthen and stabilize the central core.*

BENEFITS: *Neck, abdomen, and hips.*

1 Lie on your back, with your knees bent and your feet flat on the floor. Extend your arms out to the side of your body at shoulder level, with your palms down. Relax your spine and shoulder girdle into neutral, and let your chest soften. Engage the abdominal and pelvic floor muscles.

2 Inhale, wide and full.

3 Exhale, and roll your knees to the right, keeping your head in neutral and both shoulders connected to the floor, with the shoulder blades in neutral. Inhale.

4 Exhale, as you return your knees to the center.

5 Repeat the movement in the opposite direction. Do the exercise a total of five times in each direction.

shoulder shrugs

AIM: *To release any tension created in the shoulders during the warm-up.*

BENEFITS: *The shoulders, neck, and spine.*

3 Inhale, and lift the shoulders toward the ears.

1 Lie on your back, with your knees bent and your feet flat on the floor. Extend your arms out to the side of your body at shoulder level, with your palms down. Let your chest soften.

2 Relax your spine and shoulder girdle into neutral. Engage the abdominal and pelvic floor muscles.

4 Exhale, and draw the shoulders blades into neutral. Do the shrugs five times, increasing to a maximum of ten.

6   BeginnerExercises

Once you are comfortable with the warm ups, you can move on
to some of the beginner exercises. At first, repeat each movement
only three to five times, building up to a maximum of ten. Read
each exercise carefully and make sure you understand it before
you start. Take it gently, making sure you breathe at the right
points, and that you keep the center connected.

This section introduces the Pilates leg exercises,
which will do wonders for your hip and thigh area. Align the body
correctly by keeping the pelvis in neutral and the hips stacked
one above the other. Do not simply swing the leg or raise and
lower it aimlessly—make sure you really experience the
movement, feeling the muscle as it lifts and lowers your leg—
it helps to imagine that you are working against some form of
resistance, such as gently flowing water.

breathing

AIM: *To strengthen the central core by activating the transversus abdominus through breathing.*

BENEFITS: *The transversus abdominus, lumbar multifidus, and pelvic floor muscles.*

2 Inhale wide and full, feeling your ribcage expand and your breath going into your back and sides.

1 Lie on your back, with your knees at 45 degrees, your feet flat on the floor, hip-distance apart, and your shoulder girdle in neutral. Rest your hands palms down, one on either side of your ribcage.

3 Exhale, gently drawing up the pelvic floor and activating the TVA in and up (MVC 30%). Feel your ribcage close in and soften, as if funneling down to the hips.

4 Continue to inhale and exhale as above, focusing your attention on your breathing. At first, inhale and exhale five times, increasing to a maximum of ten.

5 Remember your breath is gentle, not forced. Exhale through the mouth, keeping the jaw relaxed, and do not be tempted to blow through pursed lips.

neutral to imprinted spine (50/50)

1 Lie on your back, with your knees at 45 degrees and your feet flat on the floor. Place your hands on your stomach, making a triangle with your thumbs in a line at the base of your navel and your fingers splayed downwards, coming together to make a point at the pubic bone (this will provide feedback as you carry out the movement). Relax your shoulder girdle and spine into neutral.

AIM: *the aim of this exercise is simply to help you position the spine into neutral when you are lying on your back.*

4 Inhale, and release the pelvis to neutral.

2 Inhale wide and full, feeling your ribcage expand and your breath going into your back and sides.

5 Exhale, and arch the back gently.

6 Inhale, and release the pelvis to neutral.

3 Exhale, engaging your pelvic floor muscles and TVA. Simultaneously draw the pubic bone toward the navel and gently tilt the pelvis toward you, rolling your tail bone off the floor. You need to identify with the position of the lower abdominals at the front of the body, from the navel to the pubic bone, so imagine this movement as a "grab" from the front, rather than a push from behind.

7 Repeat the inhale and the exhale five times each at first, increasing to a maximum of ten. Check that the pelvis has come back to neutral properly each time.

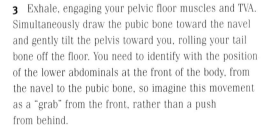

Beginner Exercises 65

lower abdominals 1

1 Lie on your back, with your knees at 45 degrees and your feet flat on the floor, hip-distance apart. Either rest your arms at your sides, palms down, or lay your hands in a triangle on your stomach as in the previous exercise. Relax your shoulder girdle and spine into neutral.

2 Inhale wide and full.

Aim: *To strengthen the central core.*

Benefits: *The lower abdominal muscles.*

3 Exhale, draw up the pelvic floor muscles and draw back the navel to the spine to 30%. Simultaneously, draw the pubic bone toward the navel and, using your abdominals, gently tilt the pelvis toward you, rolling your tail bone off the floor. As in the previous exercise, this is a "grab" from the front, not a push from behind.

4 Inhale, and hold the tilt, keeping the TVA contraction activated at 30%.

5 Exhale, as you roll back to neutral.

note

This is a challenging exercise as you need to maintain the core connection while breathing naturally. You also need to make sure you are activating the tilt from the muscles of the lower abdominals and not the gluteus maximus (buttocks).

6 Repeat the exercise five times at first, increasing to a maximum of ten. Each time, hold the position for one inhale and one exhale, keeping the abdominals scooped and hollowed. As you become familiar with the movement, you can progress to two inhales and two exhales as you hold the position, and then gradually increase to a maximum of ten inhales and ten exhales.

Beginner Exercises **67**

abdominals 1

AIM: *To flex the spine and strengthen the central core.*

BENEFITS: *The neck, shoulders, spine, and abdominals.*

1 Lie on your back, with your knees at 45 degrees and your feet in line with your knees. Rest your arms by your sides, palms down. Lengthen your neck, and relax your upper body, keeping your shoulder girdle neutral.

2 Inhale and lengthen through the back of your neck by gently nodding or rocking your chin to your chest. Do not jam your chin into your chest or raise your head—just imagine your neck lengthening on the floor.

3 Exhale, activate the pelvic floor and navel to spine (30%), then flex forward, letting your head and shoulders curl off the floor and bringing the ribcage toward the pelvis. Raise your arms off the floor, level with your shoulders. Make sure your pelvic floor muscles and TVA are engaged, navel to spine, and that your spine remains neutral. Do not lead with the head and shoulders—let the flexion come from the center.

4 Inhale, maintaining flexion. Make sure the pelvic floor stays drawn up and you maintain navel to spine. Resist the temptation to release the body back—keep focused forward, with the abdominals hollowing out.

5 Exhale, and lower and roll the body back to the floor. Repeat the movement five times at first, increasing to a maximum of ten.

leg slide

AIM: *To stabilize the pelvis.*

BENEFITS: *The center connection and the hip flexors/extensors.*

1 Lie on your back, with your knees bent at 45 degrees and your feet flat on the floor. Rest your arms by your sides, palms down and elbows slightly kinked. Relax your shoulder girdle and spine into neutral and engage the pelvic floor and navel to spine.

2 Inhale, wide and full.

3 Exhale, drawing up and back, and slide one leg away along the floor until it is fully extended, keeping the heel in contact with the floor.

4 Inhale, keeping your leg straight.

5 Exhale, draw up and back, and slide the leg back up to 45 degrees.

6 Repeat the movement five times, then change to the other leg. Increase the repetition to a maximum of ten on each leg.

progression

As you become familiar with this exercise and your stabilization improves, you can progress to alternating the legs. However, make sure that you are strong enough to do this without rocking the pelvis.

knee folds

1 Lie on your back, with your knees bent at 45 degrees and your feet flat on the floor. Rest your arms by your sides, palms down. Relax your shoulder girdle and spine into neutral and engage the pelvic floor and navel to spine.

2 Inhale, wide and full.

3 Exhale and let one knee float slowly up toward the ceiling, as if being pulled by an invisible string. Stop when the knee is in line with the hip and the angle of the knee is 90 degrees.

4 Inhale, maintaining 30% TVA activation and keeping the leg bent at 90 degrees.

5 Exhale, lowering your foot to the mat with the knee bent at 45 degrees. Do not let the back arch as you return the foot to the floor, and keep the center connected and strong.

6 Repeat the movement five times, then change to the other leg. Increase the repetition to a maximum of ten on either leg.

AIM: *To stabilize the pelvis, strengthen the lower abdominals and mobilize the hips.*

BENEFITS: *Transversus abdominus and hip flexors/ extensors.*

progression

As with the previous exercise, you can progress to alternating the legs once your stabilization improves. Make sure that you are strong enough to do this without rocking the pelvis. Be very careful not to let the abdominals dome and the back arch as you replace the foot to the floor.

flowing arms

When carrying out this exercise, it is essential that you maintain trunk organization so that the back does not arch and the ribcage does not pop off the floor. Until you have mastered the movement, only take your arm back over your head as far as it will go without losing the rib connection.

1 Lie on your back, with your knees bent at 45 degrees and your feet flat on the floor. Rest your arms on the floor beside you, palms down, but make them strong, with a slight bend in the elbows. Relax your shoulder girdle into neutral.

AIM: *To stabilize the shoulder girdle.*

BENEFITS: *The shoulders and abdominals.*

2 Inhale, wide and full, and raise one arm until it is at chest level with the fingers pointing toward the sky.

3 Exhale, engaging the pelvic floor muscles and TVA and keeping the spine neutral. Take the arm back as if to touch the floor (you may not be able to go all the way back at first). Keep the pelvis in neutral, the abdominals engaged with the ribcage, the ribs sliding toward the hip bones, and the shoulder blades melting down your back, with the shoulder girdle stable.

4 Inhale as you start to return the arm to the mid-position.

5 Exhale, and lower the arm to the floor. Repeat the movement five times, gradually increasing to a maximum of ten.

progression

Once you are confident that you are able to keep the pelvic girdle in neutral, alternate the arms, working them both together in a flowing movement, so that one arm flows up over your head as the other flows down to the floor.

trunk rotation

Aim: *To strengthen and stabilize the central core.*

Benefits: *The neck, abdomen, and hips.*

In this exercise you rotate your head in the opposite direction to your legs, being careful to maintain the shoulder connection to the floor.

1 Lie on your back, with your knees bent and your feet flat on the floor. Extend your arms out to the sides at shoulder level, with your palms up to let the shoulder blades remain in neutral. Relax your spine and shoulder girdle into neutral, and let your chest soften. Engage the abdominal and pelvic floor muscles.

2 Inhale, wide and full.

3 Exhale, and engage the pelvic floor muscles and TVA. Roll your head in one direction and your knees in the other. Exhale, and roll your knees to the right and your head to the left, keeping both shoulders connected to the floor, with the shoulder blades in neutral.

4 Inhale wide and full.

5 Exhale, as you return your knees and head to the center.

6 Repeat the movement five times to one side, increasing to a maximum of ten, then change to the opposite side.

c-curve

This is a progression of the warm-up exercise. This time, position your hands lightly on the sides of your knees. Try to unroll farther each time you practice the movement but only go as far as you can comfortably, without losing form.

1 Sit on the floor, with your weight evenly distributed over both sitting bones and your spine in neutral. Relax your shoulders, with the shoulder blades melting down your back.

2 Inhale, and sense the inflation, elongating through the spine.

3 With the points of your toes gently touching the floor, engage the pelvic floor muscles and TVA navel to spine at 30%. Connect with the center, slowly roll backwards off the pelvis. Rock slightly back and forth.

Aim: *To mobilize the spine and strengthen the central core.*

Benefits: *The spine, neck, shoulders, and abdominals.*

4 Balancing on your toes, inhale as you roll back to the start position. Repeat the movement five times, gradually increasing to a maximum of ten.

modification

Relax your feet and lift your toes, resting only your heels on the floor (this will take the tension out of your hip flexors).

spine stretch

AIM: *To lengthen the muscles of the spine.*

BENEFITS: *The neck, shoulders, spine, hips, and abdominals.*

1 Sit on the floor, with your weight evenly distributed over both sitting bones, and your legs extended hip-width apart (if the hamstrings are too tight, bend your knees slightly or sit on a rolled-up towel or mat). Lengthen your spine, so that the crown of the head is reaching toward the ceiling.

2 Extend your arms in front of you, slightly below shoulder level, palms facing up. Relax the shoulder girdle into neutral.

3 Inhale, and lengthen the spine, lifting up from the hips.

4 Exhale, engaging the pelvic floor and TVA. Curl the chin to the chest, but do not force it. Keep the abdominals scooped so that the ribs float to the hips. Curl out toward your feet as if rolling over a large beach ball.

5 Inhale as you slowly unfurl, one vertebra at a time, until the spinal column is restacked.

6 Exhale, bringing up your head and letting your shoulder blades slide back down. Repeat the movement five times, increasing gradually to a maximum reach of ten.

spine twist

1 Sit on the floor, with your weight evenly distributed over both sitting bones. Extend your legs, with your inner thighs touching, or sit in the cross-legged "tailor" position. Lengthen your spine so that the crown of your head reaches toward the ceiling. Cross your arms over your chest, and relax the shoulder girdle into neutral.

AIM: *To strengthen and mobilize the spine.*

BENEFITS: *The obliques, lumbar multifidus, transversus abdominus, and shoulder girdle.*

2 Inhale.

progression

When you are confident about your position and control, alternate the twist to one side, then the other, increasing from five repetitions each side up to a maximum of ten.

3 Exhale, engaging the pelvic floor muscles and TVA. Lift out of your hips and slowly turn to one side, using the waist.

4 Inhale, keeping the pelvic floor muscles and TVA engaged as you return to the center position. Repeat the movement five times in one direction, then repeat it five times in the other direction, making sure that the twist is initiated from the abdominals and not the shoulders.

swan dive 1

1 Lie face down, with your forehead resting on the floor on a folded towel or soft pillow. Rest your arms by your sides, palms up, and relax your shoulders into neutral. Keep your inner thighs connected and your feet pointed.

2 Inhale, lengthening through your spine and sliding your shoulder blades down your back.

3 Exhale, engaging the pelvic floor muscles and TVA.

AIM: *To strengthen and stabilize the shoulder girdle and spine, and work the spine extensors.*

BENEFITS: *The shoulders, spine, transversus abdominus, hamstring, and gluteus maximus.*

4 Inhale, peeling your upper body off the floor from the hips. Lengthen through the back, pulling your shoulder blades down. Keep the abdominals engaged for support. Keep the chest wide open and the shoulders in neutral. Keep your eyes focused on the floor and do not push back the neck and head.

5 Exhale, and lower your upper body to the floor, drawing in the navel and pelvic floor. Repeat the movement five times, increasing to a maximum of ten.

swimming

Aim: *To lengthen the spine and legs.*

Benefits: *Shoulders, spine extensors, and transversus abdominus.*

1 Lie face down, with your forehead resting on your hands and your legs extended. Relax the spine and shoulder girdle into neutral.

2 Inhale, engaging the pelvic floor muscles and TVA.

3 Exhale, and lift your left leg off the floor. Point the toes and lengthen the leg away from the body, keeping the neck long and the pelvis and ribs in alignment.

4 Inhale as you return to the start position.

5 Repeat the movement with the right leg. Repeat the whole exercise five times, increasing to a maximum of ten.

forward leg kick

The following exercises are carried out as a series, so work through them both on one leg first, then repeat them on the other leg. Repeat each movement five times at first, gradually increasing to a maximum of ten.

AIM: *To strengthen the lower back, mobilize the hips, and work the buttocks and hamstrings.*

BENEFITS: *The hip flexors, transversus abdominus, and gluteus maximus.*

1 Lie on your side with your lower arm fully extended, palm up. With the hips stacked one on top of the other, bend the lower leg into a figure 4. The top leg should be straight and hovering at hip height. Keep your top shoulder relaxed and drape your free hand and arm over your navel. Relax the shoulder girdle into neutral.

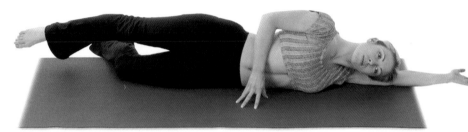

2 Inhale, and engage the pelvic floor muscles and TVA. Dorsiflex the upper foot, stretching through the heel, and draw the leg forward to 90 degrees. Maintain a neutral pelvis.

3 Exhale, plantarflex the foot, pointing the toe, and draw back the leg to its starting position, keeping the leg at hip height and maintaining a neutral pelvis.

top leg lift

Aim: *To mobilize the hips and work the buttocks and hamstrings.*

Benefits: *The hip flexors, transversus abdominus, gluteus maximus, and hamstrings.*

1 Lie on your side with your lower arm fully extended, palm up. With the hips stacked one on top of the other, bend the lower leg into a figure 4. The top leg should be straight and hovering at hip height. Keep your top shoulder relaxed and drape your free hand and arm over your navel. Relax the shoulder girdle into neutral.

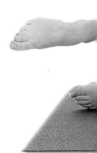

2 Inhale and engage the
pelvic floor muscles and TVA.
Plantarflex the foot and lift
the leg slightly.

3 Exhale, and lower the leg
to its starting position.

7 Intermediate Exercises

This section contains a large number of movements from the beginner exercises, but you will find that there are now subtle changes that make them a little more challenging. Each exercise has a panel explaining the purpose of the exercise, and of the progression where relevant. For some of the exercises, you will also find tips to help you support the movement until you are ready to carry it out unaided. As always, you are not looking for instant results, so do not feel you are failing if you have to call on this extra support at first.

As before, the goal is to start with five repetitions and build up slowly, adding one repetition at a time, until you can achieve ten in good form—that is, in a slow, controlled, flowing movement. Relax, find your rhythm, and remember that focus, precision, and breathing are still all-important.

breathing

As with the introductory level, start with this exercise to focus your attention on your breathing.

Aim: *To strengthen the central core by activating the transversus abdominus through breathing.*

Benefits: *The transversus abdominus, lumbar multifidus, and pelvic floor muscles.*

2 Inhale wide and full, feeling your ribcage expand and the breath going into your back and sides.

1 Lie on your back, with your knees at 45 degrees, your feet flat on the floor, hip-width apart, and your shoulder girdle in neutral. Rest your hands across your ribcage.

3 Exhale, gently drawing up the pelvic floor and activating the TVA in and up (MVC 30%). Feel your ribcage close in and soften, as if funneling down to the hips.

4 Continue to inhale and exhale as above, focusing your attention on your breathing. At first, inhale and exhale five times, increasing to a maximum of ten. Remember your breath is gentle, not forced. Exhale through the mouth, keeping the jaw relaxed, and do not be tempted to blow through pursed lips.

note

In this exercise, it is important that you relax and observe the flow of the breath as it moves in and out of the body. To help you focus, inhale to a count of four, then exhale to a count of four.

lumbar rolls

1 Lie on your back, with your knees at 45 degrees and your feet flat on the floor, hip-width apart. Relax your shoulder girdle and spine into neutral.

2 Inhale wide and full, feeling your ribcage expand and the breath going into your back and sides.

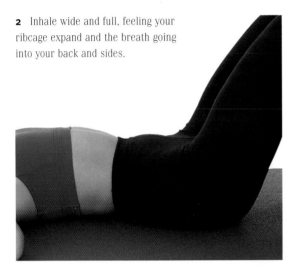

3 Exhale, engaging your pelvic floor muscles and TVA. Simultaneously draw the pubic bone toward the navel and gently tilt the pelvis toward you, rolling your tail bone off the floor.

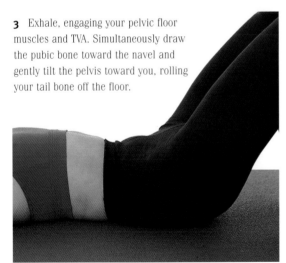

4 Inhale, and release the pelvis to neutral.

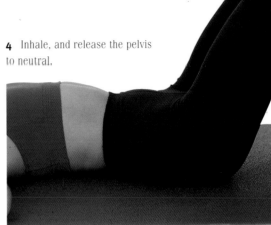

5 Exhale, and arch the back gently.

6 Inhale, and release the pelvis to neutral. Repeat the movement five times, increasing gradually to a maximum of ten.

AIM: *To strengthen the central core.*

BENEFITS: *The abdominal muscles.*

note

If you would like feedback as you carry out the movement place your hands on your stomach, making a triangle with your thumbs in a line at the base of your navel and your fingers splayed downward, touching to make a point at the pubic bone.

lower abdominals 2

In the introductory exercise for lower abdominals, you held the tilt as you inhaled. Now that you are familiar with the technique, hold the contraction—*not your breath*—for 10–20 seconds, as you inhale and exhale rhythmically.

1 Lie on your back, with your knees at 45 degrees and your feet flat on the floor, hip-width apart. Either rest your arms at your sides, palms down, or lay your hands in a triangle on your stomach. Relax your shoulder girdle and spine into neutral.

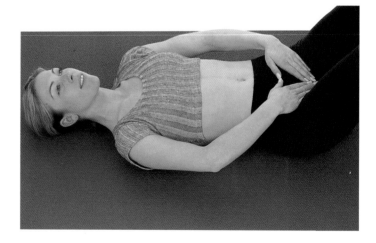

2 Inhale, wide and full.

AIM: *To strengthen the central core.*

BENEFITS: *The lower abdominal muscles.*

3 Exhale. Simultaneously draw the pubic bone toward the navel and, using your abdominals to initiate the movement, gently tilt the pelvis toward you.

4 Inhale, and hold the tilt, keeping the TVA contraction activated at 30% as you breathe rhythmically for 10–20 seconds.

5 Exhale, as you roll back to neutral. Repeat the movement five times, gradually increasing to a maximum of ten.

abdominals 2

In the introductory exercises for the abdominals, you held the flexion as you inhaled. In this exercise, you release the flexion by 5% as you inhale, and come back to it as you exhale, without touching the floor. Keep your gaze on your knees as you carry out the movement to ensure good head and neck placement. If you feel your head getting heavy, support it lightly with one hand, your elbow open wide like a wing—but do not clamp your head too hard and draw it forward.

1 Lie on your back, with your knees at 45 degrees and your feet in line with your knees, hip-width apart. Rest your arms by your sides, palms down. Lengthen your neck, and relax your upper body, keeping your shoulder girdle neutral.

2 Inhale, and lengthen through the back of your neck by slightly nodding your chin to your chest, without raising your head.

3 Exhale, and flex forward, letting your head and shoulders curl off the floor and bringing the ribcage toward the pelvis. Raise your arms off the floor, level with your shoulders. Make sure your pelvic floor muscles and TVA are engaged, navel to spine, and that your spine remains neutral.

AIM: *To flex the spine while strengthening and stabilizing the central core.*

BENEFITS: *Neck, shoulders, spine, and abdominals.*

4 Inhale, and from the flexion release your body back by about 5% so that you extend the spine slightly while still maintaining the abdominal hollow. Do NOT return to the floor.

5 Exhale, drawing up the pelvic floor and contracting the navel to spine by 5% so that you are scooped as in Step 3. Repeat the movement five times, increasing to a maximum of ten.

Intermediate Exercises   91

one hundred

This is perhaps the most well known of the Pilates movements, combining the main aims of Pilates—to strengthen and stabilize the central core while promoting controlled and rhythmic breathing. Mastering the Abdominals 1 and 2 movements will prepare you well for this exercise. In its most advanced form, the One Hundred includes gentle beats with the arms, but for stability the arms are kept strong but static here.

1 Lie on your back, with your knees at 45 degrees, your feet flat on the floor and your inner thighs connected. Rest your arms by your sides, palms down, but keep them strong, with a slight bend in the elbows. Relax the shoulder girdle into neutral.

2 Inhale, and lengthen through the back of the neck.

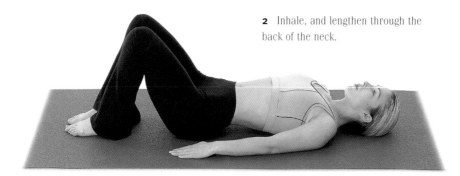

AIM: *To flex the spine, stabilize the shoulder girdle and pelvis, strengthen the central core, and promote breath control.*

BENEFITS: *The neck, shoulders, spine, abdominals, and breathing.*

3 Exhale, and flex forward, letting your head and shoulders curl off the floor and bringing the ribcage toward the pelvis. Raise your arms off the floor and keep them strong, level with your shoulders. Make sure your pelvic floor muscles and TVA are engaged, navel to spine, and that your spine remains neutral.

4 Inhale, and count to five, maintaining the TVA contraction at 20–30%.

5 Exhale, and count to five, holding the flexion and pulling the contraction to 30%.

6 Repeat the movement five times, gradually increasing to a maximum of ten. With each repetition, try to maintain the center connection and do not let the major abdominal muscle dome.

progression

Only try these variations once you are confident of your stability, as you MUST be able to keep your pelvis and spine in neutral, without arching or straining the lower back or lifting the hips.

1 Raise one foot so that the knee is at 90 degrees, directly over the hip. To do this, inhale and roll your pelvis as in Lower Abdominals 2 (page 88), then exhale and raise one leg as in Knee Folds (page 71).

2 Raise both feet so that both knees are at 90 degrees, directly over the hip. To do this, first raise one leg as above, then inhale, maintaining the position, and exhale as you raise the other leg.

bent knee circle

This is a fantastic exercise for mobilizing the hip joints, and is particularly useful if you spend a lot of time sitting down or driving so that the muscles of the hip and inner thighs are rarely stretched. When circling the knees, make sure you exhale when the leg is moving away from you, as this is when you most need stability and a good connection with the center. In its most advanced form, this movement is carried out with the leg fully extended.

1 Lie on your back, with your knees bent at 45 degrees and your feet flat on the floor, hip-width apart. Rest your arms by your sides, palms down, or place them on your stomach in a triangle for feedback—the sides of the triangle should remain even as you carry out the movement. Relax your shoulder girdle and spine into neutral.

2 Inhale.

3 Exhale, engaging the pelvic floor muscles and TVA, and take one knee up to 90 degrees, in line with the hip. Hold the position.

4 Inhale, keeping the pelvic floor muscles and TVA engaged. Circle the knee clockwise toward you to the mid-line, keeping the leg stationary— as you do this imagine you are stirring the leg in the hip socket.

5 Exhale, completing the circle by taking the knee away from you.

6 Continue, circling the knee five times clockwise and five times counter-clockwise.

7 Repeat the movement with the other leg.

progression

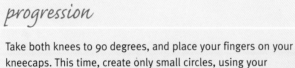

Take both knees to 90 degrees, and place your fingers on your kneecaps. This time, create only small circles, using your fingers to give you feedback that your legs are moving evenly. When circling both legs like this, it is essential to keep the pelvis stable so that the back does not arch off the floor.

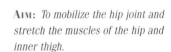

AIM: *To mobilize the hip joint and stretch the muscles of the hip and inner thigh.*

BENEFITS: *The abdomen, hips and inner thighs.*

rolling

1 Sit on the floor, sitting up on the sitting bones, with the spine flexed forward as in the C-Curve (page 75), and with the pelvis slightly tilted away, i.e. tucked under. Your knees should be bent at 45 degrees and your legs connected. Place your hands on your shins and keep your shoulders in neutral.

AIM: *Abdominal connection and spinal articulation stretch of the erector spine muscles.*

BENEFITS: *The spine, neck, shoulders, and abdominals.*

2 Inhale. Follow your pelvic tilt and C-Curve by rolling back to the floor behind you.

3 Exhale. Keep your gaze on your knees and your head in the slightly forward, C-Curve position.

variation

As a variation, try placing your palms on your calves instead of your shins. You may find this releases the tension in your shoulder muscles, enabling you to relax them and to avoid shrugging up. While learning this exercise, you can also place your feet down between rolls.

4 Keeping the center connected and the legs in line with the hands, roll back to the start, staying balanced.

single leg stretch

This exercise is a more challenging progression of the sliding leg movement (page 70). Start slowly, keeping the body flat on the floor and the legs at 90 degrees. Stretch your legs out at a pace that lets you keep your body in neutral. As you gain strength and control over the central core, flex the body before stretching out the legs.

1 Lie on your back, with your inner thighs connected, your knees bent at 45 degrees and your feet flat on the floor. Rest your arms by your sides with your palms down and a slight bend in your elbows.

2 Inhale, lengthening through the back of the neck.

3 Exhale, and initiate the pelvic tilt, engaging the pelvic floor muscles and the TVA, navel to spine, and keeping the spine neutral. Keeping the inner thighs connected, raise both knees to 90 degrees.

AIM: *To promote coordination, to strengthen and stabilize the abdominals, and to stretch the leg muscles.*

BENEFITS: *The neck, shoulders, transversus abdominus, hip flexors (eccentrically), and hip extensors and quadriceps (concentrically).*

4 Inhale, maintaining the position.

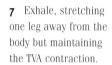

5 Exhale and flex forward, letting the head and shoulders curl off the floor and bringing the ribcage toward the pelvis. Raise your arms to shoulder level. Keep the pelvic floor muscles and TVA engaged, navel to spine, and keep the spine neutral.

6 Inhale, to prepare.

7 Exhale, stretching one leg away from the body but maintaining the TVA contraction.

8 Inhale, returning the leg to center.

9 Exhale, stretching the other leg away from the body. Repeat the exercise five times in a cycling movement, gradually increasing to a maximum of ten.

modifications

If you are unable to perform this exercise, substitute the leg slides from the Beginner Exercises, then carry on with the remainder of the exercises from this level.

double leg stretch

This movement requires a very strong and stable central core, especially as you progress. You can raise one leg at a time or both together, depending on your level of stability.

AIM: To promote coordination, to strengthen and stabilize the abdominals, and to stretch the leg muscles.

BENEFITS: The transversus abdominus, pectorals, and hip flexors (eccentrically and concentrically)

1 Lie on your back, with your inner thighs connected, your knees bent at 45 degrees and your feet flat on the floor, hip-width apart. Rest your arms by your sides with your palms down and a slight bend in your elbows.

2 Inhale, and lengthen through the cervical spine.

3 Exhale, and initiate a pelvic tilt, engaging the pelvic floor muscles and the TVA, navel to spine, and keeping the spine neutral. Keeping the inner thighs connected, raise both knees to 90 degrees.

4 Inhale, maintaining the position.

5 Exhale, and flex forward, letting the head and shoulders curl off the floor and bringing the ribcage toward the pelvis. Raise your arms to shoulder level. Keep the pelvic floor muscles and TVA engaged, navel to spine, and neutral spine.

7 Exhale, extending both arms and both legs away from the center line.

6 Inhale, to prepare.

8 Inhale, and return to the center. This exercise is very difficult and challenging, so aim for very slow and steady progress. Start with only three repetitions, then build up to five, then seven to eight, and eventually to ten.

modifications

When carrying out the modifications, flex the upper body off the floor and make sure you have a very strong, connected center. Inhale and circle your arms to the ceiling, then exhale as you draw the shoulder blades down your back, completing the circle.

The arms must be strong like a beating wing, but not tense. Your shoulders and the shoulder girdle must be stable, with the blades being drawn down as you lower the arms. This will enable you to circle (circumduct) your arms in the optimum position, without causing tension in the neck or shoulder area.

shoulder bridge

This is an ideal exercise for rolling away the stresses of the day. It is not a pelvic thrust—the aim is to roll through the spine, segment by segment. Roll only as far as you are comfortable each time, starting with the lower abdomen, then progressing to the navel, the ribcage, and eventually to the base of the shoulder blades. At the top of the position the shoulder blades must be relaxed.

1 Lie on your back, with your knees at 45 degrees and your feet hip-width apart. Rest your arms by your sides, palms down. Lengthen your neck, and relax your upper body, keeping your shoulder girdle neutral.

2 Inhale.

3 Exhale, and initiate the pelvic tilt toward the ribcage, engaging the pelvic floor muscles, TVA, and navel to spine and keeping the spine in neutral. Articulate through the spine from the tail bone, one vertebra at a time, as far as the base of the shoulder blades, so that your body forms a bridge shape. Do not roll as far as the neck (cervical spine).

4 Inhale, maintaining the TVA contraction.

AIM: *To lengthen the body and articulate through the spine.*

BENEFITS: *The transversus abdominus, the gluteus maximus, and the hamstrings.*

5 Exhale and articulate, one vertebra at a time, back to the start position, dropping the heart first, rolling into the navel, and lastly dropping the tail bone. Repeat the movement five times, gradually increasing to a maximum of ten.

spine stretch

This movement is the same as in the introductory level. However, it is essential to do this exercise at this stage, as the body needs to flex forward to balance the muscle work.

AIM: *To strengthen the abdominals and lengthen the muscles of the spine.*

BENEFITS: *The abdominals, spine, and hips.*

1 Sit on the floor, with your weight evenly distributed and your spine in neutral. Lengthen your spine so that the top of your head reaches toward the ceiling. Extend your legs, hip-width apart (if your hamstrings feel too tight, bend your knees slightly). Extend your arms in front of you, slightly below shoulder level, with the palms facing up. Relax the shoulder girdle into neutral.

2 Inhale, and lift up out of the hips, elongating the spine.

3 Exhale, engaging the pelvic floor muscles and TVA. Curl the chin to the chest, but do not jam it. Let the ribs float down to the hips, keeping the abdominals scooped. Curl out toward your feet as if rolling over a large beach ball.

4 Inhale as you slowly unfurl, one vertebra at a time, until the spinal column is restacked.

5 Exhale, bringing your head up last as your shoulder blades slide down your back. Repeat the movement five times, gradually increasing to a maximum of ten.

spine twist

This is a wonderfully relaxing exercise. Imagine yourself as a corkscrew, exhaling as you draw up and twist, and inhaling as you unwind back to the center. At first, work one side at a time, keeping the pace even and making sure the sitting bones remain on the floor. As you progress, you can work from one side to the other in a flowing movement. A further progression is to hold the twist on the exhale, then push round a little farther before inhaling and returning to the center in one movement.

3 Exhale, engaging the pelvic floor muscles and TVA. Lift out of your hips and slowly turn to one side, using the abdominal contraction to initiate the movement as if drawing the navel in lateral rotation.

1 Sit on the floor, with your weight evenly distributed over both sitting bones and your spine in neutral. Lengthen your spine so that the top of your head reaches toward the ceiling. Extend your legs, keeping the inner thighs connected. Extend the arms laterally, palms up. Relax the shoulder girdle into neutral.

2 Inhale.

AIM: *To work the muscles at the waistline (obliques) and the spine rotators.*

BENEFITS: *The obliques, lumbar multifidus, transversus abdominus, and shoulder girdle.*

4 Inhale, maintaining the pelvic floor and TVA contraction as you return to the center position. Again, initiate the movement from the center as if drawing the navel toward the mid-line.

5 Repeat the movement five times one way, then repeat five times the other way. Gradually increase the repetitions to a maximum of ten. When you are confident that the pelvis is stable, alternate the twists.

swan dive 2

Positioning your hands at shoulder level in the progression exercise will help stabilize you and enable you to peel your upper body farther off the floor, but maintain control in the center and resist the temptation to push up on your hands. The shoulders must stay in neutral and the ribs and pelvis must remain integrated to ensure that the ribs do not move forward, taking the abdominals with them.

1 Lie face down, with your forehead resting on the floor on a folded towel or soft pillow. Rest your arms by your sides, palms facing out, and relax your shoulders into neutral. Keep your inner thighs connected and your feet pointed.

2 Inhale.

3 Exhale, engaging the pelvic floor muscles and TVA and lengthening through the spine.

4 Inhale, peeling your upper body off the floor from the hips. Lengthen through the back, pulling your shoulder blades down. Keep the abdominals engaged for support. Keep the chest wide open and the shoulders in neutral. Keep your eyes focused on the floor and do not push back the neck and head.

AIM: *To strengthen and stabilize the shoulder girdle and spine.*

BENEFITS: *The shoulders, spine, transversus abdominus, hamstring, and gluteus maximus.*

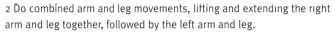

progression

1 When you have achieved good form working the upper body, extend both arms together, with the shoulder blades relaxed and in neutral.

2 Do combined arm and leg movements, lifting and extending the right arm and leg together, followed by the left arm and leg.

3 Cross-combine arm and leg movements, first lifting and extending the right arm and left leg together, then by the left arm and right leg.

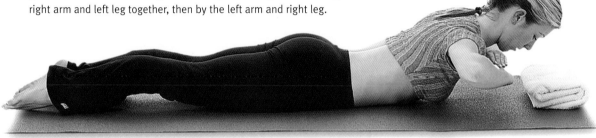

5 Exhale, maintaining the connection with the center, and lower the body to the floor. Repeat the movement five times, gradually increasing to a maximum of ten.

swimming

AIM: *To lengthen the spine and strengthen and stabilize the center.*

BENEFITS: *The transversus abdominus, shoulder stabilizers, and spine extensors.*

If you have a back or hip problem, seek advice before attempting this exercise as bilateral movement can exacerbate some conditions. Take the exercise slowly, as it requires good central stability while the arms and legs are pulling away from each other.

1 Lie face down, with your forehead resting on your hands, and your legs relaxed, hip-width apart. Relax the spine and shoulder girdle into neutral.

2 Inhale, engaging the pelvic floor muscles and TVA.

3 Exhale, and lift your left leg off the floor. Point the toes and lengthen the leg away from the body, keeping the neck long and the pelvis and ribs in alignment.

4 Inhale as you return to the start position.

5 Repeat the movement five times with the left leg, then five times with the right leg. Gradually increase the repetitions to ten. When you feel confident that your legs and pelvis are stable, alternate the legs for a total of six to ten repetitions (that is, raising each leg three to five times).

6 Inhale, engaging the pelvic floor muscles and TVA.

7 Exhale, and extend the right arm in front of you. Keep your head in line with your arm, your shoulder blades melting down your back and your neck long. There should be no tension in the upper body—as you extend one arm, keep the other folded to aid stability.

8 Inhale as you return to the start position. Repeat the movement five times with the right arm, then five times with the left. Gradually increase the repetitions to ten. When you feel confident, alternate the arms for a total of six to ten repetitions.

cat stretch

Maintain the connection to the center throughout this exercise. When you return the spine to the start position, do not let it drop or sag toward the floor—imagine yourself supporting a tray on a flat back, with the shoulders set, the head and neck in line with the spine, and the pelvis in neutral.

AIM: *To mobilize the spine and help with stabilization.*

BENEFITS: *The spine, shoulders, neck, and abdomen.*

1 Kneel on all fours, with your spine and shoulder girdle in neutral, your knees under your hips, and your hands under your shoulders.

2 Inhale and, keeping the body in neutral, engage the pelvic floor muscles and TVA.

5 Exhale and uncurl the spine from the tail bone, letting the head come back up to the start position.

6 Repeat the movement five times, gradually increasing to a maximum of ten.

3 Exhale and, keeping the abdominals scooped to the spine for support, flex the spine, curling from the tail bone toward the head and dropping your head between your arms.

4 Inhale at the top of the movement and extend the spine so your back is arched like a cat stretching. Maintain the TVA contraction.

superman

As with the previous exercise, maintain the connection to the center throughout this exercise, keeping the shoulders set, the head and neck in line with the spine, and the pelvis in neutral. It is a great challenge, as you extend the leg away, to keep the pelvis level and not drop the hip of the extended leg. If you have a problem with your knees and find this exercise uncomfortable, stop practicing it.

1 Kneel on all fours, with your spine and shoulder girdle in neutral, your knees under your hips, and your hands under your shoulders.

2 Inhale, engaging the pelvic floor muscles and TVA. Lengthen away from the center through the spine, tail bone, and crown.

AIM: *To strengthen the center and stretch and lengthen the spine and legs.*

BENEFITS: *The transversus abdominus, gluteus maximus, and hamstrings.*

3 Exhale, maintaining the abdominal contraction. Extend the right arm away from the center, in line with the shoulder and the head. Keep the shoulder girdle organized.

4 Inhale, and return to the start position.

5 Repeat the movement five times with the right arm, then five times with the left arm. Gradually increase the repetitions to ten. When you feel confident that your arms and shoulders are stable, alternate the arms for a total of six to ten repetitions (that is, extending each arm three to five times).

6 Inhale, engaging the pelvic floor muscles and TVA. Lengthen away from the center through the spine, tail bone and crown.

7 Exhale, maintaining the abdominal contraction. Extend the right leg away from the center, in line with the hip. Keep the pelvic girdle organized.

8 Inhale, and return to the start position.

9 Repeat the movement five times with the right leg, then five times with the left leg. Gradually increase the repetitions to ten. When you feel confident that your legs are stable, alternate the legs for a total of six to ten repetitions (that is, extending each leg three to five times).

progression

1 When you have achieved good form with both the legs and the arms, combine the two movements, extending the right arm and leg together, followed by the left arm and leg,

2 Combine the two movements, extending the right arm and left leg, followed by the left arm and right leg.

forward leg kick

For this exercise, the center needs to be really strong as the base of support is limited and the body will be inclined either to roll forward or rock back. So, although it is a leg exercise, keep thinking "center." You may find it helpful to place a small towel between your arm and your head for support—this will help to keep your neck in alignment with the spine.

1 Lie on your side, with your hips stacked one on top of the other and your legs together with the inner thighs connected. Extend your lower arm, palm up, so that you are in a straight line from your fingertips to your toes.

2 Now angle your legs forward slightly, without changing the position of your spine, which must remain in a straight line from your head to your tail.

3 From this position, separate the top leg and bring it back in line with your hip joint, hovering at hip height, with the foot dorsiflexed (bent upward). Keep the knee facing forward in the same direction as the hip—do not let it rotate toward the floor. Bend the upper arm at the elbow with the palm over your stomach, for feedback. Keep the top shoulder relaxed and in alignment, and the shoulder girdle in neutral. Rest your head on your arm to keep in line with the spine.

Aim: *To strengthen and stabilize the center and work the hips and abdomen.*

Benefits: *The hips, flexors, transversus abdominus, and gluteus maximus.*

4 Inhale, engaging the pelvic floor muscles and TVA. With the foot dorsiflexed, stretch through the heel. Draw the leg forward to 90 degrees, maintaining a neutral pelvis—you may not be able to achieve the 90 degrees at first, so go as far as you can without losing form and progress gradually.

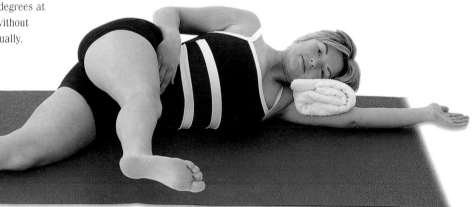

5 Exhale, plantarflex (stretch) the foot and draw the leg back to the start position, maintaining a neutral pelvis and keeping the leg at hip height. Repeat the movement five times with one leg, then turn over and work the other leg. Gradually increase the repetitions to a maximum of ten.

Intermediate Exercises   113

top leg lift

As with the previous exercise, the center needs to be really strong as the base of support is limited and the body will be inclined either to roll forward or rock back. So, although it is a leg exercise, keep thinking "center."

AIM: *To strengthen and stabilize the center, and work the hips, abdomen, hamstrings, and calves.*

BENEFITS: *Abductors of the buttocks and top leg, and transversus abdominus.*

1 Lie on your side, with your hips stacked one on top of the other and your legs together with the inner thighs connected. Extend your lower arm, palm up, so that you are in a straight line from your fingertips to your toes.

2 Now angle your legs forward slightly, without changing the position of your spine, which must stay in a straight line from your head to your tail.

3 From this position, separate the top leg and bring it back in line with your hip joint, hovering at hip height. Point your toes. Keep the knee facing forward in the same direction as the hip—do not let it rotate toward the floor. Bend the upper arm at the elbow with the palm over your stomach, for feedback. Keep the top shoulder relaxed and in alignment, and the shoulder girdle in neutral (not rounded either forward or back). Rest your head on your arm to keep in line with the spine.

4 Inhale, engaging the pelvic floor muscles and TVA. Keeping the toes pointed, slowly lift the leg up from the hip to a maximum of 25 degrees. Lengthen through the toes, as if reaching for a light switch.

5 Exhale, and at the top of the movement draw the toes toward you as you lower the leg back to the start position, lengthening through the heel as if pressing the foot into a stirrup.

6 Repeat the movement five times, keeping the leg and foot movement flowing—do not pause at the top or bottom

of the movement—then turn over and work the other leg. Gradually increase the repetitions to a maximum of ten.

circles

This movement is an excellent way to finish the leg series exercises. As with the previous exercises, the center needs to be really strong as the base of support is limited and the body will be inclined either to roll forward or rock back. Make sure you are drawing the circles from your hip, not simply wiggling your foot or toes.

1 Lie on your side, with your hips stacked one on top of the other and your legs together with the inner thighs connected. Extend your lower arm, palm up, so that you are in a straight line from your fingertips to your toes.

2 Now angle your legs forward slightly, without changing the position of your spine, which must still be in a straight line from your head to your tail.

3 From this position, separate the top leg and bring it back in line with your hip joint, hovering at hip height. Point your toes. Keep the knee facing forward in the same direction as the hip—do not let it rotate toward the floor. Bend the upper arm at the elbow with the palm over your stomach, for feedback. Keep the top shoulder relaxed and in alignment, and the shoulder girdle in neutral (not rounded either forward or back). Rest your head on your arm to keep in line with the spine.

4 Inhale, wide and full, engaging the pelvic floor muscles and TVA.

5 Exhale, and draw circles with your leg—five to the front and five backwards. Keep the circles small—imagine that your leg is inside a small jar, and that you are working around the circumference of it. Repeat the movement five times, then turn over and work the other leg. Gradually increase the repetitions to a maximum of ten.

AIM: *To work the hips, buttocks, and thighs, and promote hip mobility.*

BENEFITS: *Transversus abdominus and hip mobility.*

8 AdvancedExercises

This small batch of advanced level exercises is undoubtedly

challenging. Do not move on to them until you feel confident that

you are ready. The approach is the same as before: make slow

but steady progress and focus all your attention on each

movement. There is a lot going on here, so you will need all your

concentration, as well as controlled, rhythmic breathing.

There are two advanced arm exercises in this section,

for working the biceps and triceps—great for toning up flab. As

with the leg exercises, it is important that you really control the

movement of the arms—resist the temptation to swing them up

and down wildly. The movements are more effective if you add

weight, either by wearing proper hand weights on your wrists,

or by holding a can of soup or beans in each hand.

This final section also includes the ultimate Pilates

move—the Advanced One Hundred. When you have mastered

this exercise, you really will be ready to take on the world!

side bicycle

The leg exercises in the earlier sections can be made more advanced by adopting this side bend position of the body. It is very important that when you are in the side bend position, you do not let the ribs sink or collapse to the floor. Keep the ribs connected to a strong center, so that your body is strong from the pelvis to the shoulder.

1 Lie on your side, with your hips stacked one on top of the other and your legs together with the inner thighs connected. Extend your lower arm, palm up, so that you are in a straight line from your fingertips to your toes. Keep your head in line with your spine, with your chin forward.

2 Inhale, and as you do so place the palm of your upper hand on the floor to help press you up.

3 Exhale, and draw your lower arm in toward your body, placing the elbow directly under your shoulder and the forearm on its side, with the fingers pointed away from the body. Keep the top shoulder in neutral, and rest the arm across the navel with the hand (or fingertips as you become more proficient) on the floor for balance.

4 Now angle your legs forward slightly, without changing the position of your spine, which must still be in a straight line from your head to your tail.

5 From this position, separate the top leg and bring it back in line with your hip joint, hovering at hip height. Point your toes. Keep the knee facing forward in the same direction as the hip—do not let it rotate toward the floor.

6 With the top leg hovering at hip height, inhale as you bend the working leg back with the heel toward your buttocks, and then extend the leg forward with the knee at 90 degrees.

AIM: *To strengthen and mobilize the hips, and work the buttocks and hamstrings.*

BENEFITS: *The hips, gluteus maximus, and hamstrings.*

7 Repeat the movement five times, keeping the leg and foot movement flowing—do not pause. Keep the center connected, as the body will tend to rock forward with the weight of the extended leg.

8 Turn over and work the other leg, repeating the movement five times. Gradually increase the repetitions to a maximum of ten on each leg.

inner thigh lift

As you carry out this movement, do not just lift the leg up and down—really feel the inner thigh muscle working from the knee to the pubic bone, as if you were resisting gravity. As in the previous exercise, do not let the ribs sink or collapse to the floor. Keep the ribs connected to a strong center, so that your body is strong from the pelvis to the shoulder.

AIM: *To stretch and strengthen the inner and outer thighs.*

BENEFITS: *The abdominals and the inner and outer thighs.*

1 Lie on your side, with your hips stacked one on top of the other and your legs together with the inner thigh connected. Extend your lower arm, palm up, so that you are in a straight line from your fingertips to your toes. Keep your head in line with your spine, with your chin forward.

2 Inhale, and as you do so place the palm of your lower hand on the floor to help press you up.

3 Exhale, and draw your lower arm in toward your body, placing the elbow directly under your shoulder and the forearm flat, with the fingers pointed away from the body. Keep the top shoulder in neutral, and rest the palm of the upper hand across the navel for feedback.

4 Now angle your legs forward slightly, without changing the position of your spine, which must still be in a straight line from your head to your tail.

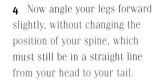

5 From this position, separate the top leg and bring it back in line with your hip joint. Bend the top leg at the knee into a figure 4. Then place the foot on the floor in front of the bottom leg, with the bottom leg fully extended.

6 Inhale and lift up the bottom leg, keeping the leg straight but without locking the knee.

7 Exhale and lower the leg without touching the floor.

8 Repeat the movement five times, without touching the floor between repetitions.

9 Turn over and work the other leg, repeating the movement five times. Gradually increase the number of repetitions to a maximum of ten on each side.

bicep curl

This exercise is for toning the upper arm to the front. The action is rather like raising the lower arm from a hinge at the elbow. For this exercise and the following one, you will need either small hand weights or two food cans of equal weight—baked beans, for example.

1 Stand with your knees slightly bent, but not locked, and your feet placed evenly under your hips. Hang your arms loosely by your sides, palms toward you. Relax your shoulders into neutral and make sure there is no tension in any part of the body.

AIM: *To work the muscle at the top of the upper arm, which flexes your arm toward your body.*

BENEFITS: *The biceps muscle.*

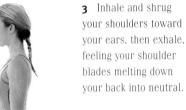

3 Inhale and shrug your shoulders toward your ears, then exhale, feeling your shoulder blades melting down your back into neutral.

4 Inhale.

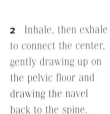

2 Inhale, then exhale to connect the center, gently drawing up on the pelvic floor and drawing the navel back to the spine.

5 Exhale and start to curl your arms at the elbows toward your body. As the lower arms move upwards, twist them so that the palms are now facing your body. At the top of the movement, your forearms will be facing your body with your palms just below the chin.

6 Inhale and lower the arms, twisting them so that your palms are facing your sides at the end of the movement.

7 Repeat the movement to make a total of ten.

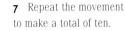

tricep kick backs

This exercise is for toning the triceps at the back of the upper arm, traditionally a slack muscle in women. Again, the elbow acts as a hinge to take the lower arm away from the body. It is essential that you keep the center connected while you are bending over, to protect the spine.

AIM: *To work the muscle at the back of the upper arm, which extends the lower arm.*

BENEFITS: *The triceps muscle.*

1 Stand with your knees slightly bent, but not locked, and your feet placed evenly under your hips. Hang your arms loosely by your sides, palms toward you. Relax your shoulders into neutral and make sure there is no tension in any part of the body.

2 Inhale, then exhale to connect the center, gently drawing up on the pelvic floor and drawing the navel back to the spine.

3 Maintaining the center connection, hinge forward from the hips. Keeping your spine in alignment, with the knees slightly bent, draw up your elbows like chicken wings. Inhale.

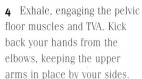

4 Exhale, engaging the pelvic floor muscles and TVA. Kick back your hands from the elbows, keeping the upper arms in place by your sides.

5 Inhale and return to the chicken wing position. Repeat the movement to make a total of ten.

advanced one hundred

This is the ultimate Pilates exercise, for which all earlier movements have prepared you. Your central stability must be 100% for this, so you will need all the core and lower abdominal strength gained from previous exercises such as Abdominals 1 and 2, Lower Abdominals 1 and 2, Lumbar Roll and Knee Folds. You must have the pelvis in neutral when performing this exercise, and the shoulder girdle set, and your back must not be flattened or arched out of its natural curves.

1 Lie on your back, with your knees at 45 degrees and your feet in line with your knees. Rest your arms by your sides, palms down.

2 Inhale, lengthening through the body and feeling relaxed.

3 Exhale, connecting the pelvic floor and drawing the navel back to the spine.

4 Inhale.

5 Exhale, maintaining the connection with the center, and raise the right leg to 90 degrees, pointing the toe.

6 Inhale, maintaining the connection with the leg at 90 degrees.

7 Exhale, reinforce the connection with the center, and raise the left leg to 90 degrees, again with the toe pointed.

8 Inhale.

9 Exhale, flexing the upper body forward with the arms extended from the shoulders and hovering above the floor. Keep the shoulder girdle in neutral with no tension. Both upper and lower body are now flexed toward the center.

10 Fully extend the legs toward the ceiling. Inhale for a count of five and maintain the position—do not let the upper body release back to the floor. Exhale for a further count of five, maintaining the connection with the center.

11 Maintain the position as you continue to breathe, inhaling for a count of five and exhaling for a count of five each time. Aim to repeat the exercise ten times, without losing form—ten repetitions by ten breaths makes the Advanced One Hundred.

single leg stretch with obliques

As with the Advanced One Hundred, you must have the pelvis in neutral when performing this exercise, the shoulder girdle must be set, and your back must not be flattened or arched out of its natural curves. Good stability at the center is essential as you are aiming for a controlled, deliberate twist using the oblique muscles, without rocking from side to side. Keep your elbows open as you perform the move, and do not be tempted to bring them in toward your head.

1 Lie on your back, with your knees at 45 degrees and your feet in line with your knees. Rest your arms by your sides, palms down.

2 Inhale, lengthening through the body and feeling relaxed.

3 Exhale, connecting the pelvic floor and drawing the navel back to the spine.

4 Inhale.

5 Exhale and let one knee float slowly up toward the ceiling, as if being pulled by an invisible string. Stop when the knee is in line with the hip and the angle of the knee is 90 degrees.

AIM: *To stabilize the pelvis, strengthen the obliques and lower abdominals, and mobilize the hips.*

BENEFITS: *Transversus abdominus, hip flexors/ extensors, and obliques.*

6 Inhale, maintaining 30% TVA activation and keeping the leg bent at 90 degrees, toe pointed.

7 Exhale, reinforce the connection with the center, and raise the other knee to 90 degrees.

8 Inhale.

9 Exhale, flexing the upper body forward with the arms extended from the shoulders and hovering above the floor. Keep the shoulder girdle in neutral with no tension. Both upper and lower body are now flexed toward the center.

10 Bring your hands to the sides of your head but keep your elbows open. Inhale, to prepare.

11 Exhale, extend your right leg away from the center, and twist at the waist to take your right shoulder to the left knee.

12 Inhale and return body and leg to the center.

13 Exhale, extend your left leg away from the center, and twist at the waist to take your left shoulder to the right knee. Repeat the exercise five times, gradually increasing to a maximum of ten.

index